Speaking Clearly

Teacher's Book

Speaking Clearly

Pronunciation and Listening comprehension for learners of English

Teacher's Book

Pamela Rogerson
Judy B. Gilbert

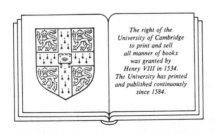

The right of the
University of Cambridge
to print and sell
all manner of books
was granted by
Henry VIII in 1534.
The University has printed
and published continuously
since 1584.

Cambridge University Press
Cambridge
New York   Port Chester
Melbourne   Sydney

Adapted from *Clear Speech* by Judy B. Gilbert
(Cambridge University Press, 1984)

Published by the Press Syndicate of the University of Cambridge
The Pitt Building, Trumpington Street, Cambridge CB2 1RP
40 West 20th Street, New York, NY 10011, USA
10 Stamford Road, Oakleigh, Melbourne 3166, Australia

© Cambridge University Press 1990

First published 1990

Printed in Great Britain by Bell and Bain Ltd, Glasgow

ISBN 0 521 31295 7 Teacher's Book
ISBN 0 521 31287 6 Student's Book
ISBN 0 521 32187 5 Set of 2 Cassettes

CE

Contents

Contents

Acknowledgements

I would like to thank all my colleagues and friends at York Language Training and Accès for their assistance and encouragement. I am also very grateful to Alec Sabin and Radio Riviera for allowing me to use their recordings.

P.R.

Introduction

This book aims to help students and teachers with an area of English which is often neglected – pronunciation. The reasons for its neglect can be various: there isn't time for it in the syllabus; teaching it doesn't seem to bring any clear results or improvements; English seems to be full of exceptions and any rules appear far too complicated; students should pick it up naturally given time. All in all, the question seems to be 'Why teach pronunciation anyway?'

There are two main reasons for teaching pronunciation: students need to understand and be understood. If they cannot understand English well they are cut off from the language, except in printed form. If they cannot be understood easily they are cut off from conversation with native speakers. This concept of intelligibility is central in pronunciation teaching, in deciding which elements of pronunciation to teach and in what order.

If students are aware of this objective of increasing intelligibility and are exposed to pronunciation as a unified system related to other aspects of the English language, such as listening, learning grammar, etc., they are much more likely to enjoy, and benefit from, pronunciation teaching.

Linguistic framework

Phonology can be divided into two broad areas: 'segmentals' referring to the individual sounds, and 'suprasegmentals' referring to sound patterns extending over a number of segmentals, e.g. intonation. Most pronunciation textbooks devote the bulk of the text to the practice of individual sounds, with a brief description of intonation at the end. As Bolinger said, referring to intonation and rhythm, 'If the child could paint the picture these would be the wave on which the other components ride up and down; but the linguist is older and stronger, and has his way – he calls them suprasegmentals, and makes the wave ride on top of the ship' (Bolinger, 1961).

This book is based on the principle that suprasegmentals are just as important as segmentals, if not more so, for achieving the objective of intelligibility.

Sequence

This book does not cover every element of English pronunciation, but concentrates on those areas which are most critical to intelligible speech. The book can be followed unit by unit, as a complete course, or the 'Pronunciation' and 'Listening' tests (on pages 2 and 109 in the Student's Book) can be used diagnostically to decide which units to give priority to. The tests can also be used to check progress at the end of each part of the book. (These tests may be photocopied.)

Integrating pronunciation teaching

There is an obvious and close link between pronunciation and listening, which is developed in this book. However, there are various ways in which pronunciation can be integrated with other language skills. For example:

Reading – 'phrasing' (marking thought groups to show which words are grouped together); picking out 'key information' (marking 'content' and 'structure' words and focus words).
Writing – spelling, punctuation.
Vocabulary – marking word stress, reduced weak vowels, classifying new items according to word stress, etc.
Speaking – all elements, especially self-assessment of recorded role-plays, etc.

Self-assessment

The 'Check your progress' section at the end of each pronunciation unit is aimed at developing students' self-assessment both by recording and critically assessing their own speech and by listening to an extract of natural authentic speech. Furthermore, the 'Further-study guide' at the end of the book should help guide and motivate students to continue their study independently.

Potential problems

At the end of each pronunciation unit in the Teacher's Book there is a 'Potential problems' section which lists some of the most likely difficulties, with examples of common language interference problems.

Cassettes

Several of the recordings are 'natural speech', i.e. authentic unscripted recordings from a variety of sources. This is so that students are exposed to the key elements of connected speech and see the important link between developing pronunciation and listening skills.

The cassette symbol 🎜 indicates that material is recorded on the cassettes.

Symbols used in the book

A line through a letter, e.g. 'banana': reduced/weak vowel.
A letter in brackets, e.g. 'Is (h)e busy?': omission of a letter.
Bars and dots, e.g. 'computer': long and short syllables.
Capital letters, e.g. 'PROduct': stress.
Underlining, e.g. 'It's my book!': focus.
Rising and falling lines, e.g. 'tomorrow' : pitch movement.

PART 1: PRONUNCIATION
Pronunciation test 😐

The Pronunciation test appears at the beginning of the Student's Book but can be used at different stages throughout the book, for either diagnostic or progress testing.

In fact, it is probably advisable to give the test diagnostically before beginning any pronunciation work, to find out where students need to improve. (You may then decide either to start at the beginning of the book, or to skip certain units or sections.) Again, the test can be used later on to measure students' progress.

When you score the test, be strict. Each section is designed to test discrimination of specific pronunciation items, so it must be clear what answer the student intends. If necessary, go through the instructions and terminology with the students before starting.

This test is recorded on the cassette. If you wish you may photocopy the pages of the text for students to hand in to you for marking.

Marking: The total score is out of 100.

Answers

A   (10 points)

1 open	........2......	4 closed	........1......
2 difficult	........3......	5 variation	........4......
3 taxes	........2......		

B   (10 points)

1 par<u>ti</u>cipant   4 pho<u>to</u>graphy
2 <u>pho</u>tograph   5 rel<u>i</u>able
3 No<u>ve</u>mber

C   (10 points)

1 bánaná   4 womén
2 womán   5 Jápan
3 Canádá

D (10 points)

1 That's i) Miss, isn't it? ....
     ii) Ms (mizz) ....✗.....
2 And you live at 22 i) Rishley Road. ....✗.....
     ii) Richley ....
3 And your name, sir, is i) Vinney, is that right? ....✗.....
     ii) Finney ....
4 And the address is 15 i) Boot Street. ....
     ii) Booth ....✗.....
5 That's in i) Axbridge, isn't it? ....
     ii) Haxbridge ....✗.....

E (10 points)

1 Oxford Circus	please be quiet	.......S......
2 Richmond Road	hurry up	.......S......
3 Victoria Station	a cup of tea	.......D.....
4 Leicester Square	answer the phone	.......D.....
5 Pall Mall	sit down	.......S......

F (20 points)

1 She doesn't <u>want to</u> do it now.
2 Please <u>give her a</u> message.
3 <u>Do you</u> think she'll come?
4 Where <u>will you</u> go?
5 How <u>long have</u> you been here?
6 <u>Is he</u> busy?
7 <u>Did you</u> call her at six?
8 What <u>have they</u> done?
9 I'm afraid <u>she's not around</u> at the moment.
10 <u>He'd have</u> told me if he'd known.

G (10 points)

A: What's the <u>matter</u>?
B: I've lost my <u>hat</u>.
A: What <u>kind</u> of hat?
B: It was a <u>rain</u> hat.
A: What <u>colour</u> rain hat?
B: It was <u>white</u>. White with <u>stripes</u>.
A: There was a white hat with stripes in the <u>car</u>.
B: <u>Which</u> car?
A: The one I <u>sold</u>!

H (10 points)

1 a) Alfred said, 'The boss is stupid.'   ....
  b) 'Alfred,' said the boss, 'is stupid.'   ....X.....
2 a) He sold his houseboat and motorbike.   ....
  b) He sold his house, boat and motorbike.   ....X.....
3 a) If you finish, quickly leave the room.   ....
  b) If you finish quickly, leave the room.   ....X.....
4 a) Pressing the pedal slowly, push the lever forward.   ....
  b) Pressing the pedal, slowly push the lever forward.   ....X.....
5 a) The passengers, who had blue boarding cards,
     were told to board the plane.   ....X.....
  b) The passengers who had blue boarding cards
     were told to board the plane   ....

I (10 points)

1 She left her glasses.   <u>statement</u>
2 He's finished.   <u>question</u>
3 The number is 35547.   <u>contradiction</u>
4 It's 22 Hills Road.   <u>contradiction</u>
5 You're English, aren't you?   <u>fairly sure</u>
6 That's his sister, isn't it?   <u>not very sure</u>
7 Really.   <u>not very interested</u>
8 Thanks.   <u>very interested</u>
9 I like the garden.   <u>enthusiastic</u>
10 The kitchen is nice.   <u>not very enthusiastic</u>

1 Syllables

Unit 1 is long because it lays an essential foundation. The notes are especially detailed, since many of the points are also useful for later units.
This unit will concentrate on:

1 Helping students understand the basic structure of syllables in English and possible vowel and consonant combinations.
2 Helping students identify the exact syllable for stress marking.
3 Helping students notice reduced syllables, such as in articles, auxiliaries, and grammatical endings, e.g. 'Where is **the** post office?'

Syllable sensitivity is important because the syllable is the basic unit of English pronunciation, and an awareness of syllables is fundamental for an awareness of other aspects of pronunciation.
Although the notion of the syllable may be universal, its structure seems to vary considerably from language to language.

A ⌞··⌟

Play the cassette or read the lists of words first vertically, then in random order. The students should tap their fingers to count the syllables. Then call on individuals to say how many syllables there are in a given word.

B

You could introduce this exercise by putting your own first name or surname on the board and asking the students how many syllables it has.
The students' names may cause disagreement. Explain, if necessary, that this is not an exact counting exercise, and avoid getting tangled in long explanations and/or arguments.
Despite what would seem to be a worrying variety of reasons for people not to get the point straight away, most students do pick up the idea rapidly. The concept is repeated regularly in the following units.

In case of difficulties, explain that an English syllable needs a vowel.
Example:

I
IN
PIN
SPIN
PINCH

The most practical solution, however, is to use tapping exercises until students intuitively perceive syllables in an English sense.

An addition to this exercise is to get the students to spell their names to you as you write them on the board. This helps check for any alphabet weaknesses and also helps you and the class learn each other's names.

Caution   Possible problems for Japanese students:

1 Japanese de-voices the vowels 'ee' (as in 'eat') and 'u' (as in 'boot') between voiceless consonants or between a voiceless consonant and silence (as at the end of a word). Therefore, a Japanese version of the name Hiroshi or Yoshiko is apt to sound like two syllables.
2 Japanese counts nasals ('n', 'm', 'ng') as syllables, with the result that a word like 'insutanto' (the Japanese version of 'instant') will sound like a six-syllable word to a Japanese!

C 😐

Answers to column 3

stupidly	3	economical	5
sentences	3	classify	3
registration	4	establishment	4
economy	4	astronomical	5

For further comparison you could use these cross-language examples of syllable number.

Spanish / English	*Japanese / English*	*Arabic / English*
clase / class	terebi / TV	lamba / lamp
chocolate / chocolate	miruku / milk	kimie / chemistry

English	cocoa (2)	*German*	Kakao (3)
		Japanese	kokoa (3)
	hygiene (2)	*Russian*	gigiena (4)
	chocolate (2)	*German*	Schokolade (4)
		Spanish	chocolate (4)

Chocolate is such a common loan word that many of the students may be able to supply a version from their languages.

D 😐

Some of your students may speak languages that do not normally have consonants at the end of words. They may feel the teacher is simply being fussy reminding them to pay attention to final consonants.

This exercise and Exercise E can help motivate students to sharpen their final consonants, by making clear the grammatical significance of their presence or absence.

Answers

1 painted	2	rented	2	added	2	caused	1
walked	1	worked	1	watched	1	started	2
landed	2	closed	1	folded	2	laughed	1

2

	Past	Present
1 They <u>start</u> at 10.00.		×
2 We often <u>rent</u> a house on holiday.		×
3 They regularly <u>visited</u> the cathedral at Christmas.	×	
4 The teachers <u>want</u> a pay rise.		×
5 I <u>intended</u> to go shopping on Saturday.	×	

3 causes	2	dishes	2	watches	2	cakes	1
rules	1	files	1	misses	2	pieces	2
mixes	2	changes	2	loves	1	prices	2

Make sure you correct any difficulties with the consonant clusters such as /dg/, /ks/, /ch/. Isolate the two sounds in each case, and get students to say the second sound first, and then add the first sound before it.
Example: e<u>xc</u>use = ex – cuse
               eks – kjus

4 1 You make amazing <u>excuses</u> when you're late.
    2 We found the most beautiful <u>beaches</u> on holiday.
    3 People usually <u>finish</u> at six o'clock.
    4 I left three <u>boxes</u> on the table.
    5 The company <u>taxes increase</u> every year.

E ☺

one syllable	two syllables	three syllables	four or more syllables
starts	castle	completed	advantages
stopped	extra	manages	interfaces
hopes	little	sentences	communication
scream	mixes		international
sport	started		
mixed	pieces		
	uses		
	support		
	managed		
	taxes		

F ☺

This exercise should make students aware that in normal fluent speech syllable boundaries are not always respected.

	Expected number	*Actual number*
1 chocolate	3	2
2 vegetable	4	3
3 comfortable	4	3
4 interesting	4	3
5 secretary	4	3
6 library	3	2

G ☺

1 The <u>roses are</u> lovely.
2 The plane <u>landed</u> at eight.
3 Petrol <u>prices increased</u> last month.
4 Did you <u>visit</u> the Mosque?
5 She put <u>her dress and blouses</u> in the suitcase.
6 They <u>wanted to rent a</u> car.
7 <u>They rented it the day before</u> yesterday.

After the dictation, ask the students to tell you the total number of syllables in the last three sentences. They are likely to be surprised by the correct number. Tap out the syllables, if necessary.

In sentence 5, check the number of syllables for 'dress' and 'blouses'. In sentence 6, the critical question is the tense of 'wanted'. It is followed by a reduced syllable 'to', making it difficult to hear correctly. In sentence 7, 'rented it the' has three reduced syllables in a row. Sensitivity to the rhythm of these three short syllables will help the listener recognise the presence of the pronoun and article, which are so frequently omitted in students' speech and writing.

Spelling is not so important here; however the word is spelt, the student should be able to read it aloud with the correct number of syllables.

Check your progress ⌐·⌐

1 It is important to encourage students from an early stage to recognise their own mistakes rather than relying on the teacher.

In the second sentence, make sure there are two syllables for 'this is' (even if the 'is' is over-emphasised) to see if the students have got a 'feel' for syllables.

2 Natural speech.

'Yes. I . . . I also worked in electronics and, er, I worked on the audio side, and, um, I basically wanted to get into recording.'

Potential problems

Students may have difficulties with some English syllables due to:

1 Lack of, or less complex consonant cluster sequences, both (a) initial, e.g. **strike**, and (b) final, e.g. **tasks**.

a) 'Initial' clusters – usually the tendency is for 'vowel insertion', i.e. to insert an extra vowel:

e.g. strike = sa-trike
    spring = si-pring

Note: Particularly with /s/ clusters.

This is common for many languages including Thai, Turkish, Spanish, Japanese.

b) 'Final' clusters – usually the tendency is for 'consonant deletion', i.e. to delete a consonant:

e.g. nest = nes
    discs = dis
    salt = sa

This is common with many languages, as above, also Hindi and Swahili.

Students may also insert vowels in final clusters:

e.g. months = 'monthiz' (Arabic)

Note: Students of some languages with a simpler syllable structure (i.e. consonant-vowel or just a vowel) may tend to insert vowels in consonant clusters in any position in the word:

e.g. strength = 'sitirenithi' (Swahili)
    steak = 'suteki' (Japanese)

2 The overgeneralisation of English syllable structure rules, such as the pronunciation of the past tense ending 'ed', especially after stops:
  e.g. stop-ped
       clim-bed
       as-ked

2 Stress

This unit aims to:

1 Introduce the concept of word stress, looking at each of the three main signals of stress (pitch change, syllable length and vowel quality) individuality.
2 Introduce the concept of 'schwa' /ə/, the most common vowel sound in English.

As in Unit 1, the concepts in this unit are fundamental for work later in the book.

Before using the book, try and elicit as much as possible from the students about what makes one syllable in a word stand out from the others. You could use the word 'chocolate' again as a cross-cultural comparison. After you have written different versions on the board, according to the nationalities in your class, ask your students to tell you which syllable has the most stress.

English – CHOColate
German – SchokoLADe
Russian – shokoLAD
Japanese – chokoLEto

Concentrate, first of all, on the fact that the voice is higher and louder on the stressed syllable in 'chocolate'.

Pitch change

If students have difficulty in perceiving pitch change, it might be helpful to use some sort of musical or kinesthetic aid (e.g. piano, mouth organ, hand gestures). Alternatively, recording the students' names and then playing them back at slow speed should help highlight the pitch change.

A

quarter	admission
career	applicant
division	application
residence	education

requirements   information
professional

B 🖭

cafeteria   orange
service   algebra
telephone   biology
theory   minister
president

Syllable length

To introduce Exercise C, you could go back to 'chocolate' and point out that the first syllable is also longer.

C 🖭

Use students' names again. A long name, like Yasumasa, is especially good for demonstrating the uneven length of syllables that is characteristic of English. First get the student to demonstrate the pitch pattern of his or her name:

Yasᴜmasa

Now you can show how English speakers typically place a pitch rise on the next-to-last syllable ('abracaᴅᴀbra'). Because pitch change and length are tied together in English (unlike many languages), the whole rhythmic pattern is altered.

Yasúmasà   Ȳasūmasà (English version)

Besides stress, which affects vowel length at the level of the syllable, there are lengthening effects at the level of the sentence (to highlight important words, see Unit 10). Because these different uses of length are likely to be new concepts for students, they should be taught one at a time. This section is important because it lays the foundation for later concepts, i.e. 'rhythm' (Unit 5) and 'voicing and syllable length' (Unit 19).

E 🖭

1 I hope you like it. I <u>designed</u> it <u>myself</u>.
2 <u>Peter's</u> not here yet. He'll be <u>along</u> in a <u>moment</u>.
3 The <u>estate</u> agent was <u>out</u>.
4 Can you <u>sign it</u> as soon as <u>possible</u>?

Vowel quality

The differentiation of strong and weak vowels is extremely important in English. Students need to know that they should not pronounce every sound clearly.

Conscientious teachers tend to enunciate every sound clearly in order to help their students understand. They pronounce the unstressed syllables just as clearly as the stressed syllables. In fact, this is the kind of English that native speakers only use when talking to foreigners. The unfortunate effect of such a model is that students find it quite impossible to understand normal spoken English. Instead of relying on structural information given to them by the rhythm of speech they rely on clear and distinct pronunciation of all vowels and consonants (Brown, 1977).

Later units will deal with the quality of consonants in stressed and unstressed syllables (Units 7 and 8). At this point, the students' attention should be drawn only to the contrast between strong and weak vowels.

Most languages are very careful to preserve the sound of each vowel in its full form. This makes the English vowel reduction system very foreign to most learners. If English is spoken with all the vowels in full form, stress patterns become confused for native listeners. One technique to show the difference is to say a word with all the vowels in strong form, then with correct combinations of strong and weak vowels. The students can practise saying the word both ways, to feel the difference.

Examples
– The word 'chocolate' can be used again. In most languages every vowel will be full. In English, the second vowel is either reduced or completely missing.

– The students' names can be analysed from the perspective of vowel quality. Typical English pronunciation:

Yasúmasá Házamá
Máriá Ortegá
Máhammád Najjár

– Write 'woman/women' on the board. Ask the students which vowel sound changes, the first or the second. At least some of the students will probably say the second. Remind them that you asked about the vowel sound, not the spelling. Despite the spelling, the second vowel sounds roughly the same in each case. This is the 'schwa' sound, which is probably the most common sound in English.

F 🔲

Nóvembér	Janúáry
Júly	Séptembér
Augúst	Apríl

G 🔲

Some students may have difficulty starting a word with a weak vowel, like 'addition'. Here are two suggestions to help them overcome this:

1 Tell students to focus on the following strong vowel, rather than on the weak vowel.
2 Get students to say the word with a preceding indefinite article or preposition, e.g. 'in addition'.

H 🔲

one strong vowel	*two strong vowels*
P<u>a</u>ris	Phil<u>a</u>d<u>e</u>lphia
Madr<u>a</u>s	C<u>a</u>sabl<u>a</u>nca
Car<u>a</u>cas	St<u>o</u>ckh<u>o</u>lm
Man<u>i</u>la	H<u>o</u>ng K<u>o</u>ng
<u>O</u>ttawa	C<u>o</u>penh<u>a</u>gen
Mil<u>a</u>n	

I 🔲

1 Three <u>women</u> were <u>arrested</u> yesterday afternoon.
2 Please send a <u>photograph</u> with your <u>application</u>.
3 My <u>sister</u> lives in <u>Buckingham</u>.
4 The official press <u>conference</u> was held in <u>Ottawa</u>.
5 <u>In addition</u>, you forgot to <u>sign it</u>.

Potential problems

Pitch change

There may be a tendency to use higher pitch on unstressed syllables than stressed syllables, particularly with speakers of Scandinavian languages, e.g. Danish, Norwegian, Swedish:

e.g. (English) ^{PE}ter   (Scandinavian) PE^{ter}

Syllable length

In some languages, vowel length makes a difference in meaning, in the same way that 'bit' and 'bet' are different words in English.

e.g. In Japanese: ȯba-sản = aunt
obaa-sản = grandmother

For native speakers of such a language, it is easy to hear vowel length differences but hard to associate this length with stress, which is its basic function in English.

Vowel length rules may be different from English (see Unit 19).

e.g. In Italian, vowels in general tend to be shorter than in English, especially in final stressed syllables and before consonants.

Vowel quality

Few languages:

1 Make such a strong distinction between strong and weak vowels as English.
2 Use weak vowels (especially 'schwa') as frequently as English.

Consequently, students may either be reluctant to use or have difficulty in using weak vowels accurately.

3 Review

This is the first of five review units in the pronunciation section of the book. The aim of these units is to consolidate the material covered in the previous units. The units can be used as quick tests either in class or for self-study.

A Syllables 😐

1 added
   mixes
   changes
   advantages

2 1 (ex)cuse me   2
   2 above   2
   3 choc(o)late   2
   4 expenses   3
   5 comf(or)table   3
   6 along the road   4
   7 p(e)rhaps   1
   8 it's on Tuesday   4

B Pitch change 😐

fan<u>tas</u>tic   <u>real</u>ly
<u>su</u>per   a<u>ma</u>zing
in<u>cre</u>dible   <u>mar</u>vellous

C Syllable length 😐

review   basis   September
around   rocket   on Thursday
arrive   answer   the last one
degree   tourist   it's lovely

Check your progress

2 ▱

    Speaker A: Where do you work? (3–4 syllables)
    Speaker B: I've got a studio, in the university. (12 syllables)

4 Word stress

This unit aims to make students aware of:

1 The importance of word stress for intelligibility (both understanding others and being understood).
2 The tendencies and rules of word stress placement (by elicitation wherever possible).

Students often underestimate the importance of word stress patterns. Incorrect stress placement is a very important cause of intelligibility problems for learners (Roach, 1983). These patterns are an essential part of the pronunciation of English and there is considerable argument for training students to learn the word stress of any new word.

There is some research evidence suggesting that native speakers store vocabulary according to stress patterns. When the wrong pattern is heard, the listener may spend time searching for stored words in the wrong category. By the time the listener realises something is wrong, the original sequence of sounds may be forgotten. For this reason, a stress pattern mistake can cause great confusion.

Warm up

You could introduce the concept of word stress, before starting the unit, by using students' names and familiar place names. Ask students to tell you which syllable is 'loudest' in each name. You can then 'misplace' the stress and get students to correct you, in order to reinforce the concept.

Rule elicitation

Rather than giving the students lists of rules, they will probably remember better if they try and discover the rules themselves.

A 😐

1 Richard Burton
 Humphrey Bogart
 Margaret Thatcher
 Ronald Reagan

2 mo**ney**   **rea**son   per**mit**
   product   **pre**sent   ma**chi**ne (odd one out)
   village   **win**dow   **wa**ter

B ⌣

Pattern: Words in the first column have stress on the first syllable, words in the middle column have stress on the second syllable and words in the last column have stress on the third syllable.

C ⌣

calcu**la**tion   de**ci**sion   re**ac**tion
so**lu**tion   distri**bu**tion   tele**vi**sion
re**la**tion   associ**a**tion   ope**ra**tion

Pattern: Words ending in 'sion' and 'tion' have penultimate stress placement.

D ⌣

bi**o**logy   bio**lo**gical   **po**licy   po**li**tical
ge**o**graphy   geo**gra**phical   uni**ver**sity   mana**ge**rial
pho**to**graphy   photo**gra**phical so**cie**ty   socio**lo**gical
tech**no**logy   techno**lo**gical elec**tri**city   e**lec**trical

Pattern: Words ending in 'cy', 'ty', 'phy', 'gy' and 'al' all have anti-penultimate stress.

E ⌣

eco**no**mic   te**rri**fic
stra**te**gic   **lo**gic
patho**ge**nic   do**mes**tic
meta**bo**lic   sta**tis**tic

Pattern: Words ending in 'ic' have penultimate stress.

F

Verb	*Noun*
pre<u>sent</u>	<u>pre</u>sent
e<u>xa</u>mine	exami<u>na</u>tion
pro<u>duce</u>	pro<u>duc</u>tion
re<u>duce</u>	re<u>duc</u>tion
re<u>cord</u>	<u>re</u>cord
in<u>sult</u>	<u>in</u>sult

Noun	*Adjective*
<u>his</u>tory	his<u>tor</u>ical
<u>sec</u>retary	secre<u>tar</u>ial
a<u>na</u>lysis	ana<u>ly</u>tical
<u>po</u>litics	po<u>li</u>tical

G

personality	antibi<u>o</u>tic
perso<u>na</u>lity	
computeri<u>sa</u>tion	<u>sur</u>gical
pharma<u>co</u>logy	<u>di</u>gital
ana<u>ly</u>tical	micro<u>sco</u>pic
agri<u>cul</u>tural	trans<u>mis</u>sion

Check your progress

2 a) Two-syllable nouns usually have stress on the first syllable.
   b) Words ending in 'ic' have penultimate stress.
   c) Words ending in 'sion' and 'tion' have penultimate stress.
   d) Words ending in 'al', 'phy' and 'ty' have anti-penultimate stress.

3
'... it's an <u>Eng</u>lish <u>Lang</u>uage <u>Train</u>ing Con<u>sul</u>tancy ... <u>spe</u>cialising in <u>in</u>dustry-spe<u>ci</u>fic <u>lang</u>uage <u>train</u>ing.'

Potential problems

1 All syllables with full vowels:
   There may be a tendency to give both stressed and unstressed syllables full vowels (i.e. vowels in unstressed syllables are not weakened), e.g. French, Indian languages, Italian.

2 Fixed word stress:
  The L1 may have fixed word stress (i.e. stress falls regularly on a particular syllable):
  – Stress on final syllable (e.g. French, Thai).
  – Stress on penultimate syllable (e.g. Swahili).

3 Variable stress placement but different rules:
  The stress placement in the L1 may not be fixed, but variable (as in English) but the rules for placement may be different, e.g. Turkish, Arabic, Italian (this may cause particular problems with cognates).

4 Only primary stress (i.e. not secondary, etc.): e.g. Russian, Greek (this may cause problems for polysyllabic words).

5 No compound word stress distinction:
  a) The distinction of compounds such as WHITE house and white HOUSE is not done by word stress but by word order (OLD book, old BOOK; libro viejo, viejo libro) e.g. Spanish, Arabic, Indian languages.
  b) Compound nouns are stressed on the first syllable (PRIME minister, FRONT door) e.g. Scandinavian, German.

5 Rhythm

This unit aims to increase students' awareness of:

1 The irregularity of English syllables.
2 The general principle that length adds emphasis.

English has a characteristic rhythm and listeners expect to hear this rhythm, i.e. it is an essential ingredient of intelligibility. It is the guide to the structure of information in the spoken message, not something added to the basic sequence of consonants and vowels (Brown, 1977).

The most important feature of English rhythm is that the syllables are not equal in duration. There is an alternation of stressed and unstressed syllables, with stressed syllables coming at regular intervals and the unstressed syllables being squeezed in between them to maintain the regular beat.

The difference in syllable length is largely related to differences in the length of vowels. Basically, there are three different lengths:

a) Reduced (e.g. bélow).
b) Full vowel, unstressed (e.g. WINdow).
c) Full vowel, stressed (e.g. baNAna).

(*Note:* When two full vowels follow each other they tend to be lengthened even more.)

English rhythm, however, is not based only on varying syllable lengths but on sentence emphasis effects. The two levels (syllable timing and sentence emphasis) are very different. For instance, English and Spanish behave very similarly in terms of sentence emphasis but there is a difference at the level of syllable timing which gives a difference in the rhythmic impression of the two languages.

It is common to refer to languages as falling into one of two distinct rhythmic groups, i.e. *stress-timed* (like English or Russian) or *syllable-timed* (like Japanese or Yoruba). However, it may be more accurate to make a distinction between *regular syllable* languages and *irregular syllable* languages.

A

As with word stress patterns it is advisable to try and encourage the

21

students to be as analytical as possible rather than merely getting them to repeat or mimic words and phrases with English rhythm.

1 Can't stop now. (regular)
2 Come here quick! (regular)
3 Come and give me a hand. (irregular)
4 That young man looks ill. (regular)
5 That old woman looks lovely. (irregular)
6 Whizz gets out dirt fast. (regular)
7 All soap makes clothes clean. (regular)
8 Whizz will do your washing quickly. (irregular)
9 Don't drink tap water. (irregular)
10 Turn the tap off. (irregular)
11 John can't come yet. (regular)
12 John can't have come yet. (irregular)

C

The strongly metrical nature of limericks, verses, songs, etc. is useful when working on rhythm. Students should, eventually, realise that they need to use the correct emphasis and pauses, and consequently, reductions and contractions, to maintain the correct rhythm.

The students should first of all listen to the recording of the limerick and concentrate on the emphasised words, before oral practice. During oral practice, the teacher can clap or tap the rhythm to make sure the students keep the regular beat. Alternatively, the class could be divided into halves, each half taking alternative lines. Another technique for any rhythm practice is to whisper it; this concentrates the mind on timing rather than pitch patterns. ('There was': the verb 'to be' is not usually stressed. The stress on 'was' here is to keep the rhythm of the limerick.)

Once again, a deductive approach should be encouraged, for example by getting students to supply the last line of a verse, using the correct rhythm.

D ☺

computerisation   he works at the station
interruption   shocked the nation
addition   the action
clarification   who did she mention
communication   another option

E 😐

Any song or poem can be used to demonstrate the difference between strong and weak vowels. Carolyn Graham's *Jazz Chants* (1978) is a good source of practice.

This chant can be read either in pairs or two groups, taking parts 'A' and 'B'. The important thing is to keep the rhythm going, for instance by clapping or using a metronome.

Check your progress 😐

'... er, many people feel that if the question is not as an important issue er, as it appears on the surface, then something should be done very rapidly...'

Potential problems

1 All syllables are the same length:
   In the L1, unstressed syllables are not reduced and squeezed in between stressed syllables. Therefore, a word with four syllables will be twice as long as a word with two syllables,
   e.g. Hi-ta-chi (Japanese) HiTAchi (typical English rhythm);
   Spanish – all vowels have the same length.

2 In the L1, the difference between stressed and unstressed syllable length may be less pronounced and all vowels are strong and full, e.g. French, Arabic, Turkish.

6 Basic sentence stress

This unit aims to:
1 Make students aware of the distinction between 'content' words and 'structure' words.
2 Make students aware of the relationship between sentence stress and meaning (i.e. information structure).

Many non-native speakers of English do not distinguish clearly enough between words which are emphasised and words which are not. Ignorance of the basic pattern of English emphasis not only adds an element of confusion to the students' speech, but also means the student is missing important signals in listening comprehension.

The distinction between a content word and a structure word is essential to English. You can help students become aware of the difference by asking them what kind of words they would put in a telegram. If they have to pay for every word, they will naturally choose the words that carry the most information. These are generally the content words. Another helpful way to think of the difference is to describe content words as 'picture words'. You can visualise 'book', 'green' or 'run', but it is difficult to picture words like 'is' or 'if'.

You can help Japanese students recognise the difference between content and structure words by mentioning the difference between the *kana* and the *kanji* characters in written Japanese. The *kana* (characters representing syllable sounds) are generally used to 'spell' structure words. The *kanji* (characters representing whole ideas) are generally used to convey content words.

One good way to illustrate emphasis is to use a highlighter pen to mark content words.

Word list

When students have tried to make a list of content words and structure words, go over it with the Summary on page 30 in the Student's Book.

B

1 Can I <u>have</u> a <u>coffee</u> and a <u>cup</u> of <u>tea</u>, please?
2 Would you <u>like another</u> one?

3 <u>Thanks</u> for a <u>lovely meal</u>.
4 <u>Sorry</u> but I <u>can't come</u> on <u>Monday</u> because I'm <u>working late</u>.
5 I've <u>never been</u> to a <u>car rally</u>.
6 I <u>usually visit</u> my <u>parents</u> on <u>Tuesdays</u>.

C

Suggested sentences (there are other possibilities):

1 I confirm the arrival of order number 235/SA.
2 Could you please contact me because I have an urgent message.
3 We regret the delay, which is due to a ferry strike.
4 I will be arriving at Milan airport on Tuesday at nine o'clock.
5 The conference has been postponed, so please cancel the flights.

D ☒

1 Chris, can you <u>contact Mrs Williams before five</u> o'clock. It's <u>urgent</u>.
2 Look Chris, I <u>need</u> the <u>report</u> on <u>Wednesday</u>.
3 Could you <u>send</u> the <u>invoice</u> to the <u>Accounts Department</u>, please, Chris.
4 Chris, I'm afraid I <u>can't go</u> to the <u>meeting</u> on <u>Friday</u>. I'm <u>too busy</u>.

Check your progress

1 A: <u>What's</u> the <u>matter</u>?
  B: I've <u>lost</u> my <u>keys</u>.
  A: <u>Where</u> did you <u>put</u> them?
  B: If I <u>knew</u>, I could <u>find</u> them!

2 ☒
  A: In fact, even in the Soviet Union they have the same problem,
     they've got now, in fact, er there's a divorce for every three
     marriages.
  B: So is it true then if you're talking about different cultures that
     perhaps something like religion doesn't come into this ... ?

Further practice

As well as telegram messages, another useful source for further practice is
expanding newspaper headlines, e.g. BOY SIX FOUND SAFE.
   Students can be asked to expand the headline into a complete sentence
and mark the content and structure words. Also, students could write their

own headlines. Such activities should help to reinforce the connection between content words being stressed and carrying important information.

Potential problems

Although most languages seem to make some sort of distinction between 'content' words and 'structure' words, this distinction does not necessarily have the same effect on speech as in English. For instance, if:

1 There is not the same relationship between stress placement and meaning, e.g. Japanese does not use intonation to highlight information structure as we do in English.

2 Structure words are not stressed but also are not reduced (see Unit 7, Reductions and contractions), e.g. Arabic and Indian languages.

7 Reductions and contractions

In the previous units students have been introduced to the basic concepts of word stress, rhythm and sentence stress and should therefore be prepared for the introduction of reductions and contractions. However, it is probably a good time to do a quick review of these points before starting this unit.

This unit aims to:
1 Introduce the concept of simplification of sounds in natural, rapid speech.
2 Consolidate awareness of the link between unstressed words and reduced or deleted vowels and consonants.
3 Develop recognition and production* of weak forms.
4 Develop recognition (and optional production) of contractions.

* It is considered important that students actually learn to produce weak, reduced forms, otherwise an excess of full vowels and stressed syllables will be very confusing for the listener. However, although contractions are commonly used in speech (but not writing), lack of use of contractions will not normally cause such comprehension difficulties, e.g. omission of 'er' in 'perhaps'.

Reductions

A

After doing the exercise with the cassette, get the students to do it again, in pairs, testing each other.

B

If students have difficulty omitting the 'h' for the reduced pronouns, tell them to say the final consonant of the preceding word,
e.g. When did (h)e go there?
        'didee'

1 a) Did (h)e go?   4 a) Give (h)im the pen.
2 a) Is (h)e here?   5 a) Is (h)er work good?
3 b) Leave (h)er alone.

Contractions

E

1 I have got a cold.
2 Do you think he has gone?
3 Where have they been?
4 I have to do some shopping.

5 We have got to work hard.
6 She has three children.
7 Have you seen John?
8 I have never been to Japan.

F ⌣

A: Hello, George. This is Sylvia. Can I speak to Jane?
B: Oh hello, Sylvia. Yes, of course. **She'll be** with **you** in a minute. **She's** just come in **and she's** taking **her** coat off. By the way, John and Barbara called **and** said **they're** going **to** Portugal next week. **They** said **to** tell you **they'll** be calling **to** see **if you're** all right **after your** operation.

G ⌣

Both contracted forms are acceptable in informal speech. Which one you choose is largely a matter of style.

1 A: Haven't you finished that report yet?
  B: Well no, I've not quite finished it.
2 A: I didn't see Steve yesterday.
  B: No, he's not got back from France yet.
3 A: Do you think Susan has left already?
  B: No, she wouldn't have gone without telling you.
4 A: I'm afraid we won't be able to make it this evening.
  B: That's a pity. Couldn't you get a baby-sitter?

H

1 No, I do not think she has.
2 I am tired. I think I will go to bed.
3 Maybe they will.
4 He is sure you are.
5 They would help you if they could.
6 No, I should not imagine he is.

I 😐

Written message:

Dear Mr Norlin,
Thank you very much for your invitation to the Geneva conference. I would be delighted to participate.
    You asked me if I would like to contribute a paper and, of course, I would be very happy to do so. Unfortunately, I can't give you the final title as I have not yet received the conference outline, but I will send you details as soon as I can.
    It is a pity I did not get to see you when I was in Paris. If I had known you were there too I would have contacted you. However, I am sure we will see each other sometime before the conference.
Yours sincerely,
P. D. Wright

Text:

Secretary: I'll read it back to you. Dear Mr Norlin...
    Thank you very much for your invitation to the Geneva conference. I'd be delighted to participate. You asked me if I'd like to contribute a paper and, of course, I'd be very happy to do so. Unfortunately, I can't give you the final title as I haven't yet received the conference outline, but I'll send you details as soon as I can. It's a pity I didn't get to see you when I was in Paris. If I'd known you were there too, I'd've contacted you. However, I'm sure we'll see each other sometime before the conference. Yours sincerely, P. D. Wright

J 😐

1 pólice	6 córrect
2 sécretáry	7 pótato
3 pérhaps	8 comfórtable
4 vegétable	9 I'm áfraid so
5 éxcuse me	10 bécause

K 😐

1 tex(t)books	4 he mus(t) be ill
2 nex(t) week	5 he aske(d) Paul
3 three-fif(th)s	6 she look(ed) back quickly

Check your progress

⌐··⌐

2 A: How've you been keeping since I last saw you?
  B: Not so bad. I've been away, actually. I've been over to Sweden for a
     couple of weeks...
  A: And you've had no problems since I last saw you?
  B: None at all. No, I think everything's OK.

Further practice

1 Again, you can use rhymes and poems to illustrate reductions and weak
  forms, e.g. 'This is the house that Jack built', and dialogues, as in
  Elements of Pronunciation by Colin Mortimer.
2 Students can be asked to find written and spoken examples of common
  reductions and contractions, e.g. 'fish'n'chips', '(ex)cuse me'.
3 Give mini-dictations, like Exercise F, and blank out the structure words.

Potential problems

1 Lack of weak forms and 'schwa' vowels in the mother language may
  cause difficulty in both perceiving and producing reduced forms, e.g.
  Japanese, Chinese, Italian, Spanish.

2 Fewer weak forms than in English, which could lead to characteristic
  overstressing of words like 'and', 'but', 'the', etc., e.g. Scandinavian,
  Dutch.

3 Fewer, or different, contractions and deletions, which may cause
  difficulty adapting to English 'rules', e.g. French (deleted 'e' – 'dev(e)l-
  opper'; contracted negative 'ne' – je (ne) sais pas).

8 Linking

There is some research evidence to suggest that non-native speakers of English do significantly less linking than native speakers. Furthermore, linking is a major source of intelligibility problems for learners of English. This unit aims to make students aware of:

1 Rules for linking in English.
2 Frequency of linking in English.

The unit moves on to deal with another aspect of the simplification of connected speech. Regular reference to preceding units should help students see the development from one element of pronunciation to another.

Some mention has already been made at the end of Unit 7 about sound changes and deletions at word boundaries (see Summary). This could be used as a starting point to introduce the concept of linking, i.e. the fact that words are not spoken separately but are linked together in some way, either by 'sound mergers' (e.g. goo(d) boy, i(m) Paris) or by 'sound insertions' (e.g. no(w) other, I(y) ought).

Introductory sentences:
a) 'I think, first of all, we ought, to ask him.' (10 words)
b) 'Is he busy on Monday evening?' (6 words)

Consonant–to–vowel

B

A: Can‿I help you, sir?
B: Yes, I'm‿in‿a rush‿I'm‿afraid. Can‿I have‿a piece‿of‿apple cake please, with‿ice cream?
A: Certainly, sir. I'll‿ask the waiter to come‿over‿as soon‿as possible.

Back-chaining

The students should practise this dialogue and the one in Exercise D by listening and repeating short phrases at a time and gradually piecing them together, backwards, as on the recording.

D 😐

A: Switch off the light, David. It's almost eleven.
B: I'm scared of the dark. I think I heard a noise. Look over there! Something on the window ledge is moving!

Vowel–to–vowel

E 😐

A: How often do ᵂI have to do ᵂit?
B: You ᵂought to do ᵂevery exercise once a week.
A: Do ᵂI have to do ᵂ*every* exercise?
B: Yes, it should take you ᵂabout two ᵂhours. Though ᵂ I don't suppose it will!

F 😐

A: Actually, I ʸought to practise more regularly ʸI suppose.
B: Well, don't worry ʸabout it. I ʸoften forget myself.
A: Perhaps we ʸought to try ʸand go together.

G 😐

A: How's it going, Edward?
B: Not bad at all. It's not exactly a busy place though.
A: Where are you staying?
B: Just a little pub on the ʸedge of town.
A: And what are you doing on your own?
B: Not a lot actually. This evening there's a match on TV, so ᵂI'll get a snack in town and watch a bit of football afterwards.

Potential problems

1 No linking from final consonant to initial vowel:
Some languages tend to insert a glottal stop before a word beginning with a vowel. This makes the speech sound jerky, e.g. Arabic, Chinese, Thai, German.

2 Vowel insertion after final 'b', 'd', 'g':
  These sounds are strongly released and are often followed by a short
  vowel, which disrupts English rhythm and linking rules, e.g. 'big' –
  'bigger' (Italian, Greek). Similarly, the strong release of final 'p', 't', 'k'
  can prevent some linking by French speakers.

9 Review

A Stress patterns

Column 1	Column 2
RElative	absoLUtely
parTIcipate	staTIstic
PHOtograph	ecoNOmic
alTERnative	indiCAtion
Agency	photoGRAphic
arguMENtative	soLUtion
technoLOgical	meCHAnic
manaGErial	
phoTOgraphy	

In column 1 the stress is on the third syllable from the end (i.e. anti–penultimate). In column 2 the stress is on the second syllable from the end (i.e. penultimate).

C Basic sentence stress 😐

1 Dialogue:
   A: Are you <u>ready</u>?
   B: <u>Not quite</u>.
   A: <u>Put</u> your <u>coat</u> on.
   B: <u>Just</u> a <u>minute</u>. <u>Don't rush</u> me!

2 Song:
   <u>Good evening. This</u> is your <u>Captain</u>.
   We are <u>about</u> to <u>attempt</u> a <u>crash landing</u>.
     <u>Please extinguish all cigarettes</u>.
     <u>Place</u> your <u>tray tables</u> in their <u>upright, locked position</u>.
   Your <u>Captain says</u>: <u>Put</u> your <u>head</u> on your <u>knees</u>.
   Your <u>Captain says</u>: <u>Put</u> your <u>head</u> in your <u>hands</u>.

D Reductions/contractions and linking 🔲

Dictation:
1 Is he busy this afternoon?
2 You ought to tell him about it.
3 It could've been someone else.
4 Give her the report you've written.
5 You shouldn't have said so.

10 Sentence focus 1

This unit aims to help students:
1 Recognise the focus of information in messages.
2 Highlight important information in messages.

As an introduction to this unit, refer students back to the Summary of basic sentence stress in Unit 6 to review the concept of putting stress on the words that carry the most information.

This unit takes this notion of information structure one step further by introducing the idea of focus, i.e. highlighting the listener's attention on different parts of messages. Focus helps to contextualise messages, i.e. it helps the listener relate something to what has been said before and to predict what is likely to be said next.

e.g. A: Where do you <u>live</u>?
     B: In <u>Brixton</u>. Where do <u>you</u> live?
     A: <u>I</u> live in Brixton <u>too</u>.

Which words are focussed depends on which words the speaker considers are important for the listener to notice. This, in turn, depends largely on whether the information is being introduced for the first time, as at the beginning of a conversation (see the word 'live' in the first line of the dialogue above), or has been mentioned before (like 'live' in the second line).

When starting a new topic or introducing new information, the focus tends to fall on the last content word in a sentence (see the first examples in the Student's Book, page 45).

If the focus is on only one word we say it is 'narrow', however it is possible to extend the focus to more than one word (see the second examples in the Student's Book), in which case we can say that the focus is 'broad'.

Emphasis on the focus word then, highlights the contrast between new and old information. All languages have one or more ways of doing this, but English relies on stress for this purpose more than most of our students' languages. For this reason, learning to hear this emphasis is both difficult and important. Students typically miss spoken signals of contrast with something said or assumed previously. When they learn to notice this signal and recognise the implications, they make a major step forward in listening comprehension.

D

A: Hello. What's <u>new</u>?
B: <u>Nothing much</u>. What's new with <u>you</u>?
A: I'm going to <u>the States</u>.
B: <u>East</u> coast or <u>West</u> coast?
A: <u>West</u>. I want to visit <u>San Francisco</u>.

E

A: Do you think British food is <u>expensive</u>?
B: Not <u>really</u>.
A: Well, <u>I</u> think it's expensive.
B: That's because you eat in <u>restaurants</u>.
A: Where do <u>you</u> eat?
B: At <u>home</u>.
A: I didn't know you could <u>cook</u>?
B: Well, actually, I <u>can't</u>. I just eat <u>bread and cheese</u>.
A: That's <u>awful</u>!
B: <u>No</u>, it <u>isn't</u>. I <u>like</u> bread and cheese.
A: You're <u>crazy</u>!

Check your progress

2

A: So is it <u>true</u> then, if you're talking about the <u>different cultures</u> that perhaps something like <u>religion</u> doesn't come into this...?
B: Well, <u>no</u> I think it's <u>not</u> so much a question of <u>religion</u>. I think you've got <u>two</u> points which need to be made.

Potential problems

1 Problems will probably arise for students whose first language does not share with English the use of stress and intonation to highlight information structure, e.g. Chinese, Japanese, Thai.

2 There may be fixed sentence focus in the L1, and therefore difficulty seeing the placement of focus as a question of speaker choice, e.g. Italian, Spanish (where the focus is usually on the last stressed syllable in a sentence).

11 Sentence focus 2

This unit aims to develop students' awareness of shifting focus for contrastive purposes, so that they can:

1 Follow the thread in discussion, arguments, etc.
2 Increase or decrease the force of their own speech.

The concept of focus is extended into more complicated language use. It is extremely important, although difficult, for students to begin to think of words not simply as they relate to sentences, but as they relate to the whole discourse structure. Consequently, all the exercises in this unit are based on conversational interaction.

Conversations are a series of exchanges of information and ideas between speakers. Speakers can communicate many different things, e.g. they may want to state, or deny, a fact strongly; give, or disagree with an opinion, etc. There are different ways of manipulating language to express these various meanings, such as using particular words and phrases, e.g. 'personally', 'to be honest', or changing word order, e.g. 'It was Jane who told me' (rather than 'Jane told me'), 'Cheese is what I like' (rather than 'I like cheese').

Another way of giving special meaning is by using stress to give contrastive focus.

Correcting information

B

Customer: Can I have <u>one cheese sandwich</u> and <u>two ham rolls</u>, please?
Waiter: That's <u>one</u> ham sandwich ...
Customer: No, one <u>cheese</u> sandwich.
Waiter: Sorry, that's <u>one cheese</u> sandwich and <u>two ham</u> sandwiches.
Customer: No, two ham <u>rolls</u>.
Waiter: Right ... You did want <u>two</u> cheese sandwiches, didn't you?
Customer: No, I <u>didn't</u>. Just <u>one</u>.
Waiter: Oh. I think I'd better <u>write</u> this <u>down</u>.

C

1 A: <u>Were</u> you in the bank on Friday?
  B: No, I <u>wasn't</u>.
2 A: Were <u>you</u> in the bank on Friday?
  B: No, but my <u>sister</u> was.
3 A: Were you <u>in</u> the bank on Friday?
  B: No, but I was <u>near</u> it.
4 A: Were you in the <u>bank</u> on Friday?
  B: No, but I was in the <u>post office</u>, next door.
5 A: Were you in the bank on <u>Friday</u>?
  B: No, but I was there on <u>Thursday</u>.

D 🔲

2 Policeman: Now Miss, do you <u>usually</u> go to the bank on Friday?
  Reply (b): Yes, <u>every</u> Friday.
3 Policeman: Did you <u>see</u> the robbers?
  Reply (a): No, but I <u>heard</u> them.
4 Policeman: And did <u>you</u> sound the alarm?
  Reply (b): No, someone <u>else</u> did.
5 Policeman: Were there <u>three</u> men?
  Reply (a): No, I think there were <u>two</u>.

Checking information

E 🔲

1 A: I didn't <u>go</u> on Friday.
  B: You didn't <u>go</u>?
2 A: He's been <u>promoted</u>.
  B: <u>Promoted</u>?
3 A: I found your keys in the <u>kitchen</u>.
  B: In the <u>kitchen</u>?
4 A: Have you seen my <u>purse</u> anywhere?
  B: Your <u>purse</u>?
5 A: The France/Scotland match has been <u>postponed</u>.
  B: <u>Postponed</u>?

F 😐

2 querying
3 querying
4 confirming
5 querying
6 confirming
7 querying

Dialogue:

B: Hello, Paul. Did you have a good holiday?
P: Yeah, it was great.
1 B: I <u>thought</u> you'd have a nice time.
P: Mm ... ended up in Italy though.
2 B: I thought you were going to <u>Spain</u>.
P: Yeah, but Jane doesn't like Spain much.
3 B: But I thought you were going with <u>Maria</u>.
P: Well, it got a bit difficult.
4 B: Mm, I rather <u>thought</u> there might be problems.
P: So anyway, I went to Florence.
5 B: I thought you'd <u>been</u> there.
P: Yes, I have but I like it. Anyway, I speak the language, you know.
6 B: Yes, I <u>thought</u> you spoke Italian.
P: Well, I must be going, Barbara. We must have a drink together sometime soon.
7 B: Yes, but I thought you were coming to my <u>party</u> on Saturday.
P: Oh, of course, I almost forgot. See you on Saturday then.

Check your progress 😐

1 A: Oh, I'll have to go and get the paper.
B: <u>I'll</u> get it for you.
2 A: When can I collect the photographs?
B: I'm afraid they won't be ready until <u>Tuesday</u>.
3 A: I'm glad you're coming on Friday.
B: But I <u>can't</u> come.
4 A: Can you finish that by five o'clock?
B: But I've <u>already</u> finished it.
5 A: What did you think of the film?
B: Well, I thought it was <u>rather boring</u>.

Potential problems

1 As in the previous unit, the main problems will probably be for students whose L1 does not use stress and intonation in this way, but uses, for example, word order, instead, as in Italian, Portuguese, Spanish, e.g.
Roberto arriva alle nove. (Roberto arrives <u>at nine</u>.)
Alle nove Roberto arriva. (Roberto <u>arrives</u> at nine.)

2 Repetition of focus on the same word:
Unlike English, it is possible to repeat the focus on the same item, as in Portuguese, Indian languages, e.g. It was <u>her</u> book not <u>her</u> bag.

12 Review

This unit aims to review the work done in the previous units on sentence emphasis and focus.

Go through the Summary with the students as a review exercise, first. Elicit more examples from them wherever possible.

A Basic sentence stress ⊡

1 The <u>Queen</u> is <u>visiting Sydney</u> this <u>morning</u>.
2 Do you <u>want</u> a <u>cup</u> of <u>tea</u>?
3 Can you <u>tell</u> him I <u>called</u>?
4 I'm <u>sorry</u> to <u>trouble</u> you but it's <u>rather urgent</u>.

B Focus ⊡

1 The film was <u>fantastic</u>!
2 Are you <u>coming</u> to the <u>party</u> on <u>Saturday</u>?
3 Can you <u>give</u> it to him?
4 I <u>think</u> I <u>left</u> it in the <u>bedroom</u>.

C New focus ⊡

A: <u>What</u> are you <u>doing</u>?
B: I <u>came</u> to <u>see Peter</u>.
A: Well, <u>Peter's not here</u>.
B: I can <u>see</u> he's not here. Where <u>is</u> he?
A: I don't know <u>where</u> he is.
B: <u>Not</u> very <u>friendly</u>, <u>are</u> you?
A: <u>Neither</u> are <u>you</u>!

D Contrastive focus 😑

1 A: Peter is <u>funny</u>.
  B: He isn't <u>funny</u>. He's <u>strange</u>.
2 A: So, the number is <u>35487</u>.
  B: No, it's 35<u>1</u>87.
3 A: That's £<u>3.15</u> altogether.
  B: £3.<u>50</u>?
  A: No, £3.<u>15</u>.

13 Thought groups 1

This is the first of two units on thought groups. This unit continues the theme of information structure in speech, but moves on from stress placement to pause and pitch movement (intonation).

The unit aims to help students:
1 Recognise and produce thought groups.
2 Be aware of some of the functions of thought groups in English, i.e. using thought groups to clarify complex sentences (e.g. restrictive v. non-restrictive clauses), and mark main and subordinate clauses.

In the last two units, on sentence focus, we looked at how to focus the listener's attention on the most important parts of a message. In this unit we will concentrate on how to show which words go together by dividing speech into thought groups, i.e. a sequence of words with one idea or thought. If we do not divide speech up into clear thought groups or 'chunks' then the listener may have difficulty understanding messages.

In English there are four main signals for marking thought group boundaries:
1 Pause
2 Pitch change
3 Interrupted rhythm
4 Lengthening of final syllable

In terms of teaching, the first two signals, i.e. pause and pitch change, are the most accessible for classroom use. However, it needs to be pointed out that in natural rapid speech pauses are not always used to signal thought groups and listeners may have to rely on pitch change alone.

A ⌐⊡¬

You can use variations of the following techniques for additional practice.
1 Dictate phone numbers and addresses from a phone book. Put the answers on the board so that students can check their accuracy.
2 Students dictate their own 'number sets' to each other in pairs (phone numbers, car registrations, passport numbers, etc.).

D ⌷

1 $(2 + 3) \times 5 = 25$	6 $(4 - 2) \times 5 = 10$
2 $2 + (3 \times 5) = 17$	7 $4 - (2 \times 5) = -6$
3 $3 \times (3 + 5) = 24$	8 $(6 \div 2) \times 5 = 15$
4 $(3 \times 3) + 5 = 14$	9 $(16 \div 4) \times 2 = 8$
5 $(3 - 2) \times 6 = 6$	10 $16 - (4 \times 2) = 8$

F ⌷

1 a)	4 a)
2 b)	5 a)
3 b)	

G ⌷

Make sure the students get plenty of oral practice with these exercises, working in pairs, and maybe making their own dialogues.

A: <u>Alison is leaving work</u>, so I've been told.
B: Really!
A: Don't tell anyone, but ... <u>she's been sacked!</u>
B: No!
A: <u>Her husband,</u> who's over there talking to Jean, <u>is very upset about it.</u>
B: Oh dear.
A: <u>They're moving</u>, so they say, <u>to the south.</u>

H ⌷

Practise filling pauses with common hesitation phrases: 'you know', 'well', 'I mean', etc. This can be helpful in preparing students to hear actual colloquial speech where these phrases are common. It might be useful to point out that most of the time these phrases are empty of meaning and that their function is only as fillers, or to encourage some response from the listener.

2 We had one or two little problems.
3 Not really, it's just the living room carpet.
4 They were painting in the kitchen.
5 And I went to answer the phone.
6 When I got back they were in the living room, painting the carpet.

Check your progress

2 ⌷⌷

'Thank you very much Patrick. And his number again, 93 98 20 58. Do get in touch with him there or you can call us here on 19 39 184 29 09 34. And Patrick Middleton's number again, 93 98 20 58.'

Further practice

'Mini-talks'. Either you or a student starts to talk about a topic, and the other students have to try and find the best time to interrupt. The speaker can use fillers to try and keep going and the students have to listen carefully for thought group signals.

Potential problems

All languages have to segment speech into manageable chunks, but not all languages use intonation (or the same intonation signals) to do it.

1 A common problem in many languages is the tendency to keep the pitch high in mid-sentence, rather than use low pitch as in English, e.g. When he arrived ↑ at the house ↑ he found that Susan ↑ was out (as in German, Scandinavian languages, French).

2 Some languages use clause-final particles (affixes) and therefore do not need to rely on intonation or timing to indicate group boundaries, e.g. Cantonese, Korean.

3 Many languages, although they use pauses for this purpose, put boundaries in different places, e.g. Turkish, Japanese, Spanish.

14 Thought groups 2

This unit aims to give students further practice and a wider understanding of the importance of demarcating thought groups, particularly in connected speech.

The recorded material illustrates three different types of speech:

1 Scripted monologue (lecture on 'Thought group markers')
2 Scripted monologue (radio news broadcast)
3 Unscripted dialogue (authentic interview between a training manager from British Telecom and a language training consultant)

It must be stressed to students that they are listening to the recordings for a very specific and limited purpose, i.e. the tasks laid out in the exercises, and not to get general information regarding content.

This unit, necessarily, simplifies the role of prosody in spoken discourse, but generally follows the research done by Crystal 1975, Brown and Yule (1983), Sacks et al (1974) and others working on conversational analysis.

Key
↑ high pitch
↓ low pitch
/   short pause
// longer pause

A 😐

If students have difficulty initially in hearing the pauses and pitch rise/fall, stop the cassette at pause boundaries to 'chunk' the speech mechanically and use hand movements to illustrate pitch movement.

B 😐

' ↑ each language has special ways to mark thought groups / but in English / the chief marker / is intonation // ↓ '

C 📼

1 '/ the listener can get confused /'	No
2 '/ you know that a lot of English sentences are very complicated /'	Yes
3 '/ today I want to tell you about some useful research /'	No

D 📼

The aim here is to help students chunk speech into thought groups, and it should be particularly helpful for less fluent students. Make sure they do not omit the high and low pitch points.

E 📼

You may want to pre-teach some vocabulary, e.g. 'assassinated', and possibly introduce the topic before you use the recording. Again, use techniques explained in Exercise A if necessary.

If you think it is too difficult for some students to speak at the same time as the cassette, get them to say the phrases without the recording.

F 📼

1 'He was shot several times'	No
2 'He was shot several times at close range'	No
3 'He was shot several times at close range and died shortly afterwards'	Yes
4 'The murder took place yesterday evening when Mr Palme was walking through the streets of central Stockholm with his wife'	No
5 'The gunman, who has not yet been identified'	No

G 📼

There are five different topics.

News bulletin:
'The Swedish Prime Minister, Mr Olof Palme, has been assassinated. He was shot several times at close range and died shortly afterwards. The murder took place yesterday evening when Mr Palme was walking through the streets of central Stockholm with his wife, after a visit to the cinema. The gunman, who has not yet been identified, escaped in the crowd.

Mrs Thatcher will be making a full statement to the Commons this afternoon. This morning she gave her first reaction to the news describing the murder as barbaric, vicious and terrible. "I shall miss Olof Palme very deeply," she said.

Now the other news. A policeman has died after a shooting incident in the centre of Manchester. Another was wounded. The gunmen escaped in a car, which it is understood has now been found abandoned.

The two sides in the ferry dispute have arrived at the London offices of the conciliation service ACAS for another attempt to end the strike.

There have been more anti-government protests in the Nigerian capital, Lagos. Twenty-eight people were injured, including fifteen policemen.

The Norwegian government has arrested three members of Greenpeace, the international environmental organisation. The captain and two crew members of the Greenpeace ship were escorted ashore after an incident involving damage to a Norwegian whaling vessel off the coast of northern Norway.

ITC radio news.'

H ⌣

Dialogue:

Diana: Oh, Chris, it's about the visitors ... ↑
Chris: Yes? (*adding something else*)
Diana: They're coming on Thursday. ↓
Chris: Right. (*finished*)
Diana: They should get here in the afternoon ... ↑
Chris: Yes? (*adding something else*)
Diana: At about 3.30. ↓
Chris: Right. (*finished*) Who exactly is coming?
Diana: Well, there's Mr Nakashi and Mr Misoko ... ↑
Chris: Yes? (*adding something else*)
Diana: And Miss Lin. ↓
Chris: Right. (*finished*)
Diana: They're staying at the Hotel Concordia ... ↑
Chris: Yes? (*adding something else*)
Diana: It's not a particularly nice hotel ... ↑
Chris: Yes? (*adding something else*)
Diana: But it's all we could get at such short notice. ↓
Chris: Right. (*finished*)
Diana: So, anyway, I'll pick them up at the airport on Thursday. ↓
Chris: Right. (*finished*)

I ⊡

Dialogue:

Training Manager: and of course we're in constant / touch with them by telephone // ↓

Interviewer: Yes / ↑ tell me / er / some of the sorts of problems that you / er / get and that would call for a / visit from / THQ // ↓

Training Manager: Er / well ↑ one of the problems would be / where we discover that something has gone wrong ...

J ⊡

1 'Good / ↑ how many / er / visits to schools would you make /' No

2 'It's difficult to say /' No

3 '... and sometimes we find that we're out of the office / er / for two or three days every week /' No

4 '... and then there may be a period when / we're / in the office for perhaps two or three weeks at a time / without going outside of London / other than for perhaps the odd meeting within the THQ / department in London // ↓ ' Yes

15 Pitch range

This unit looks at another aspect of intonation, pitch range (i.e. the scale of pitch movements between the upper and lower limits of the voice). It aims to:

1 Give students practice in using an extended pitch range.
2 Make students aware of the relationship between pitch range and interpretation of the speaker's meaning.

For native English speakers, the normal pitch range seems to be between 80 and 300 c.p.s. (cycles per second) (Brown and Currie, 1980) but most of the time we keep within the lower half of the scale, unless we want to show greater involvement in what we are saying (e.g. surprise, enthusiasm, strong disagreement, etc.).

As well as individual variations in pitch range, there are variations between languages (Tomatis, 1966), both in the pitch range itself and in the functions of pitch range.

A

1

2

3

4

5

6

7

8

9

Dialogue:

Peter: Sarah, I'm going to a party tomorrow night, would you like to come?
Sarah: Oh.
Peter: It's just an office party really.
Sarah: Oh.
Peter: But it's at the Grand Hotel.
Sarah: Oh.
Peter: And there'll be a marvellous meal.
Sarah: Oh.
Peter: And live music.
Sarah: Oh.
Peter: It's for Mr Lucas, you know, he's retiring.
Sarah: Oh.
Peter: But there'll be some younger people there too ...
Sarah: Oh.
Peter: ... like the new accountant ...
Sarah: Oh.
Peter: ... Miss Peacock. They say she's very nice ... but a bit quiet.
Sarah: Oh.
Peter: So, what about it? Are you going to come?
Sarah: Er ... I'm not sure Peter ...

B ▱

Interested in	Not interested in
Planetarium	British Museum
Buckingham Palace	Trafalgar Square
Hyde Park	Covent Garden
Oxford Street	
Leicester Square	

Dialogue:

Travel agent: You really must visit the Planetarium. It's fantastic.
Customer: Really.
Travel agent: And then there's the British Museum.
Customer: Oh yes.
Travel agent: And, of course, there's Buckingham Palace. You can't miss that.
Customer: Oh.
Travel agent: You can walk through Hyde Park.
Customer: Yes.
Travel agent: And see all the shops in Oxford Street.
Customer: Yes.

Travel agent: And go to a theatre in Leicester Square.
Customer: Really.
Travel agent: And look at the fountain in Trafalgar Square.
Customer: Mm.
Travel agent: But there are lots of other things to do as well, like visit the market at Covent Garden and ...
Customer: Yes. Well, thank you very much but I think that's enough for now.

C

The man is more enthusiastic than the woman.

Potential problems

1 There may be a narrower pitch range in the first language, so that the voice tends to sound flat or too even in English giving the impression of being impolite or uninterested, e.g. Spanish, Greek, French.

2 Pitch range may vary between the sexes, so attempts to impose an English use of pitch range may cause embarrassment or reluctance, e.g. In Japanese, only women use higher pitch to signal politeness (men use much lower pitch).

16 Pitch curves

In this unit we will look at another aspect of intonation – pitch curves (i.e. the direction or movement of pitch in speech). The unit aims to:

1 Give students practice in recognising and using the two basic pitch curves in English (i.e. rising and falling).
2 Make students aware of some of the functions of falling and rising pitch curves, particularly in questions.

It should be pointed out to students that we are looking at some common tendencies for intonation in English and that they are not expected to learn, or mimic, a set of fixed intonation patterns or rules.

Furthermore, while there are some intonation universals (which should help students to use systems from their own language), there are also many regional variations within English which make it difficult to talk about 'rules'.

Examples:
A: There's no hot water. (falling)
B: There's no hot water. (rising)

Getting information

A

1 Why do you smoke?
2 What's it for?
3 How do you spell it?
4 Who's he with?
5 How often do you go?
6 Has she finished yet?

The pitch is rising on 6 and falling on the others. Point out that 'WH' questions frequently end with falling pitch.

B

The pitch curves on Pat's questions:

Hello, my name's Pat. Would you like a drink?
Are you English?
Where exactly are you from?
Oh, really, and have you been here very long?
Oh, I see. Are you studying here?
Oh, yes. Where are you staying by the way?
Really, is it far from here?
Mm. Well, I'm afraid I must be going. It's been nice talking to you. Bye.

Checking information

C 　

The exercises give practice in distinguishing between 'open' and 'closed'
situations.

'Open' situations generally use rising pitch, to signal that something is
incomplete, unresolved or open for negotiation.

'Closed' situations generally use falling pitch, to signal that something is
definite, finished or confirmed.

The difference is well illustrated in 'tag' questions, where tags ending
with falling pitch signal that the speaker has a certain expectation about
what the answer will be, i.e. the speaker expects confirmation of his or her
statement. Tags ending in rising pitch, however, suggest that the speaker is
less sure about the answer to his or her statement, i.e. is open to
negotiation.

Asking for repetition

D 　

Again, this exercise illustrates some differences between 'open' and 'closed'
situations.

Dialogue 1
'How many'? has rising pitch because speaker A has either not heard or
not understood the previous reply.

Dialogue 2
'Forty?' has rising pitch because speaker A does not consider the exchange
'closed' – he is either doubtful or surprised.

Dialogue 3
'Forty' has falling pitch because speaker A is now 'closing' the exchange,
i.e. he is confirming the previous reply.

c

Check your progress

2 ⌗

Dialogue (I = Interviewer, D = Dave):

I: Dave, what exactly do you do?   *(getting information)*
D: I'm a recording engineer.
I: Yes.   *(checking information)*
D: Yes.
I: What sort of work do you get involved in?   *(getting information)*
D: Um, mainly bands, recording erm groups, er voices, sound effects, er but most, most of the work is in recording groups.
I: And do you end up with the finished product?   *(getting information)*
D: Yes.
I: Yeah, so you take the work from the beginning to the end?   *(checking information)*
D: Yes.
I: Yeah? How long have you been doing this sort of work?   *(getting information)*
D: Er, two years now.
I: Two years. And what did you do before that?   *(getting information)*
D: Before that, I was a musician.
I: Really! What, what instrument do you play?   *(getting information)*
D: Guitar and bass guitar.
I: Ah. Is that how you became interested in recording?   *(getting information)*
D: Yes. I, I also worked in electronics, and, er, I worked on the audio side, and, um, I basically wanted to get into recording.
I: You're interested in the technical side of it?   *(checking information)*
D: Yes, as well, as well as the musical side.
I: Yeah. Do you still play your guitar?   *(getting information)*
D: Yes.
I: Professionally?   *(getting information)*
D: Yes.
I: Ah. Have you made any recordings of yourself?   *(getting information)*
D: Er, I've been on a few records. I've been on television a lot.
I: Great.

Potential problems

Difficulties are most likely to arise where either intonation does not have the same functions in the first language or the intonation curves are different, so that features of the first language carried over into English sound inappropriate,

e.g. Chinese – pitch change is associated with syllables rather than
      complete words and phrases.
      Russian – 'Yes/no' questions have falling pitch (Has she done it?).
      Portuguese – all tag questions end in rising pitch (You're English,
      aren't you?).

17 Review

This unit aims to review the work done in previous units on thought groups, pitch range and pitch curves.

Check your progress ⌣

A: This is / in fact one of the differences / between the school systems ↓ / isn't it?
B: ... ↑ What about when children change / from English to French / and back to French ...?

Further practice

Choose several short extracts of natural speech, e.g. news broadcasts, to analyse in the same way.

Similarly, it is a good idea to get students into the habit of analysing their own speech, by recording short talks, dialogues, etc., and seeing how much use is made of these intonation features.

18 Voicing

This section of the book deals with some basic English sound contrasts, in particular those contrasts which seem to cause most difficulties for students.

It aims to help students (a) perceive, and (b) produce voicing contrasts in English.

General guidelines for teaching sound contrasts

1 Decide which sound contrasts you need to work on (you can use the Diagnostic tests in Units 23 and 24 to help you).

2 Try to develop and increase *perception* of the sounds. Students may not 'hear' or 'perceive' the sound because:
   a) The phoneme* does not exist in their own language, e.g. / ɪ / in French.
   b) The sound exists but not in the same positions as in English, e.g. /b/, /d/, /g/ at the end of words in German tend to sound like /p/, /t/, /k/ respectively, so 'pig' may sound like 'pick'.

   To develop perception of sounds make sure the students have plenty of opportunity to hear the new sounds, both in a 'narrow' context (i.e. in 'minimal pairs'†) and in a 'broad' context (i.e. in sections of natural speech).

3 Practise *production* of the sounds, remembering:
   a) Not to demonstrate or ask learners to produce sounds in isolation, but to put them in the context of a syllable, word or phrase.
   b) Not to expect students to follow technical instructions about the mechanics of the vocal organs (apart from obvious parts like 'lips', 'teeth' and 'tongue').
   c) It is usually easier for students to produce a new sound in initial position, i.e. at the beginning of a word, and then move on to practising it in final position and, finally, in mid position.

4 Develop, as quickly as possible, the concept of 'self-correction'; getting students to correct themselves and each other. This helps increase their own perception and their motivation.

---

* 'Phonemes' are the meaningful sound segments of a language, that is the 'building blocks', e.g. /p/, /ʊ/, /t/ in 'put'.
† 'Minimal pairs' are pairs of words which differ only in one phoneme, e.g. 'put' and 'pit'.

In a study of English as a Second Language pronunciation errors (Leahy, 1980) it was found that the two main types of errors were based on 'voicing' (<u>z</u>oo / <u>S</u>ue, see Units 18 and 19) and 'continuancy' (bu<u>s</u> / bu<u>t</u>, see Unit 20).

In voicing errors, the problem with stop sounds was found mainly in the final position (cap / cab) and was directly related to the length of the preceding vowel (see Unit 19). The voicing errors with continuants occurred in all positions, not just finally (<u>s</u>ink / <u>z</u>inc, bu<u>s</u> / bu<u>zz</u>, ser<u>v</u>ice / sur<u>f</u>ace).

Voicing refers to the vibration of the vocal cords when a sound is made, giving the sound a 'buzzing' quality. Apart from pressing the fingers against the ears, another way of hearing voicing is to put a hand on the front of the throat so that you can feel a slight vibration.

B

1 zap	zap	<u>sap</u>	zap
2 fan	<u>van</u>	fan	fan
3 service	<u>surface</u>	service	service
4 advice	<u>advise</u>	advice	advice
5 <u>teethe</u>	teeth	teeth	teeth
6 riding	riding	<u>writing</u>	riding

C

1 The fan won't start.	(b) Take it to an electrician.
2 Zip it carefully.	(b) Why? Is it broken?
3 I don't like writing.	(a) Well, phone her instead.
4 This surface is terrible!	(a) Yes, be careful, it's very slippery.
5 Can't you try it later?	(b) OK. Maybe the line is busy.

Potential problems

(See 'General guidelines' on page 59.)

Problems may arise either because sounds do not exist in the L1 or do not occur in the same position in a word:
e.g. /θ/ and /ð/ – in Arabic, German, French, Chinese, Japanese (students may substitute /s/ and /z/);
/f/ and /v/ – in Japanese and Chinese;
/z/ – in Chinese, some Spanish (students may substitute /s/).

19 Voicing and syllable length

This unit aims to extend students' awareness of voicing and the relationship between voicing and syllable length.

Begin by asking students what the difference is between the verb 'use' and the noun 'use'. The answer has two parts: (a) voicing of the final consonant, (b) length of the vowel:

'use' (verb) – lengthened vowel, voiced consonant
'use' (noun) – shortened vowel, unvoiced consonant

The lengthened vowel helps the listener identify the consonant. Do the same exercise with 'loose' (adj.) and 'lose' (verb). Students may expect 'loose' to be longer, because it looks longer in print.

A ⊡

2	1	ice	ice	eyes	ice
	2	cab	cab	cab	cap
	3	peas	peace	peas	peas
	4	bag	back	bag	bag
	5	rich	rich	ridge	rich

B ⊡

2 1 advise (verb)
   2 use (noun)
   3 close (verb)
   4 loose (adjective)
   5 proof (noun)

C ⊡

1 There's something in my ice.	(b) Call a waiter.
2 I thought I heard a buzz.	(a) It's only a fly.
3 Is that your cap?	(b) No, mine is brown and checked.
4 I sent Diana flowers.	(b) Did she like them?

Potential problems

1 In the L1 sounds may not be voiced at the end of words,
e.g. /b/, /d/, /g/ may sound like /p/, /t/, /k/ at the end of words in
German, Turkish.

2 Some voiced sounds may not exist at the end of words,
e.g. in Chinese, /b/, /d/, /g/, exist in initial position but not final,
therefore, students may substitute /p/, /t/, /k/.

20 Stops and continuants

This unit aims to help students: (a) recognise, and (b) produce stop and continuant sounds.

First of all, review the concept of 'voicing' from the previous two units by putting the letters 'p', 't' and 'k' on the board and asking if they are voiced or not. Then ask for their voiced equivalents, i.e. 'b' 'd', and 'g'.

Explain that you are now going to look at another important sound contrast in English and introduce the concept, of 'stops' and 'continuants' with the 'is' and 'it' exercise in the Student's Book.

Again, refer back to the 'p', 't' and 'k' on the board and ask if they are stops or continuants. Try testing several unfamiliar words, like 'dedication'. Just say the word, without writing it down. Analyse the word, syllable by syllable, checking the consonants with questions like: 'Is it voiced?' 'Is it a stop?'

It is advisable to avoid words with a consonant cluster, since this might lead to a confusion (e.g registration). Students could be asked to find and analyse one or two words of their own in this way.

Once students have a physical sense of the difference between stops and continuants, the contrast can be used to clarify a number of sound problems.

A ⌣

1 1 Do you like <u>soup</u>?   (a)
  2 What are you <u>washing</u>?   (b)
  3 That's a <u>fine</u> bed.   (a)
  4 The teacher <u>thought</u> for a long time.   (b)
  5 Have you seen that <u>ram</u> over there?   (b)

2 1 Tip it slowly.   (b) It's too heavy!
  2 I like ships.   (b) I don't, I get seasick.
  3 What's the date today?   (a) The fifth of November.
  4 The bet cost me £20.   (a) Well, you shouldn't gamble.
  5 Is it red?   (a) No, it's orange.

B 😐

1 The words in column 1 end in continuant sounds.

D 😐

I like those blac<u>k</u> boots but I thin<u>k</u> tha<u>t</u> whi<u>te</u> jacke<u>t</u> looks ghastly!

Note: These reductions may be subject to regional variations. However, the main point in this exercise and the previous one is that stops are often unreleased in 'difficult' consonant clusters.

Potential problems

1 Difficulties with /r/:
   Although /r/ is a continuant in English, it sounds like a brief stop in many languages, because the tip of the tongue taps or trills against the roof of the month, e.g. Japanese, Spanish, Arabic.

2 Difficulties with the contrast 'sh' and 'ch':
   Point out that the 'ch' begins with a stop sound ('t' + 'sh'), e.g. French, Italian.

3 Confusion between 'yet' and 'jet':
   Use the same method to show that the 'y' is a voiced continuant and the 'j' has an initial stop sound 'd' before the 'zh' sound of mea<u>s</u>ure, e.g. Scandinavian languages, Spanish.

4 Difficulty recognising and producing 'v':
   If students are substituting a sound like 'b', point out the stop/continuant distinction, e.g. Spanish, Japanese.

5 Difficulty distinguishing 'tank' and 'thank':
   Again, point out the stop/continuant distinction, e.g. French, Italian, Chinese.

21   Puff of air (aspiration)

This unit looks at another sound contrast which is a common cause of errors for students. It aims to help students discriminate between aspirated and unaspirated sounds, e.g. between 'p', 't', 'k' and 'b', 'd', 'g'.

The sounds 'p', 't' and 'k' are followed by a slight puff of air before a following vowel. This 'release' of air is a distinctive element of these sounds in English; if listeners do not hear this aspiration they will probably hear the sounds as 'b', 'd' and 'g'. Furthermore, for many students, it is an easier way of differentiating the stops rather than trying to clarify the voicing differences (pole/bowl). It is easier to practise and may be easier to hear. A Spanish speaker named 'Perez', for example, probably has difficulty getting an English speaker to understand the spelling of the name. Even if the 'p' stop is said without voicing, sound is likely to be judged a 'b', unless the aspiration is heard.

Apart from the paper technique, another way of helping students produce aspiration is to get them to make an 'h' straight after the stop and before the vowel,

e.g. 'pit'
    'p' + 'hit' = p(h)it

    'pen'
    'p' + 'hen' = p(h)en

C   😐

1 1 I want to <u>try</u> this T shirt. (a)
    2 My friend's name is <u>Bobby</u>. (b)
    3 What beautiful <u>curls</u>! (a)
    4 What a strange looking <u>coat</u>. (b)
    5 Have you seen that <u>drunk</u>? (a)

2 1 Is it gold?   (a) No, it's silver.
    2 The pub is very noisy.   (a) Let's go to another.
    3 What a lovely beach.   (b) Yes, just look at the sand.
    4 Where's the path?   (b) At the end of the village.
    5 I hate bills.   (b) Yes, I never pay them unless I really have to.

Potential problems

Any language groups that do not have the same voicing and/or aspiration sound contrast,
e.g. Arabic – 'bebsi' for 'Pepsi'
      Turkish – 'budder' for 'butter'
      Russian – 'bit' for 'pit'
Also Turkish, Spanish, Italian, French.

22 Review

This unit reviews the work done in the previous units on:

a) voicing and syllable length;
b) stops and continuants;
c) aspiration.

To add variety and interest to the exercises an element of competition could be introduced in the class with students either working in pairs or teams. For example, in Exercise A they could ask each other if the final sound in the word they say is voiced or not voiced. Similarly, for Exercise C, they could say words from the list at random and ask if they are aspirated or not. Exercise B could be extended by asking students to produce sentences of their own incorporating as many stop/continuant contrasts as possible, e.g. /tʃ/ and /ʃ/.

23 Sound contrasts – Consonants

This unit looks at some English consonants which cause difficulties for students in many language groups. It aims to help students: (a) perceive differences between some common consonant sound contrasts, and (b) correct inaccurate sounds.

Before starting the unit it is advisable to refer to the 'General guidelines for teaching sound contrasts' at the beginning of Unit 18 (on page 59).

Diagnostic test ▱

This test can be used as an introductory guide to students' difficulties. The test can be done either at the beginning of this unit or at the beginning of Unit 18.

Dialogue:

A: I think his name is Vane, John Vane.
B: No, it's not, it's Wane.
A: Oh well, I think the next one is Liddle, isn't it?
B: Yes, that's right. And then, the next one is Varley, I think.
A: No, I think that's a 'B' for Barley.
B: Oh yes, so it is.
A: What about this, can you read it?
B: Difficult, but it looks like Foulton to me, Anna Foulton.
A: Mm, yes. This next one is easier ... Litham, Eric Litham.
B: Right. What's next? Is that Siegler?
A: Looks more like Ziegler to me.
B: OK.
A: And this one is Chepstow, I think.
B: Yes, I think you're right.
A: I can't read the last one at all!
B: Terrible writing, isn't it. I think it must be Arlington, though.
A: So, that's Sue Arlington. Good, that's it then.

1 Wane
2 Liddle
3 Barley
4 Foulton
5 Litham

6 Ziegler
7 Chepstow
8 Arlington

1 'th' / 't'

B

	Continuants	Stops
Voiced	there	dare
	these	bad
	clothes	din
	that	
	breathe	
Unvoiced	teeth	toes
	month	
	breath	

If students have problems producing the 'th' sounds, ask them to put the
tip of their tongue either between the teeth or touching the back of the
front teeth and push the air out through the mouth at the same time.
Explain that for a 't' sound the tongue briefly touches the hard ridge just
behind the front teeth (the 'tooth ridge' in the diagrams).

3 'sh' / 'ch' / 'j'

B

1	2	3
shoes	cheque	jam
shells	cheese	major
sugar	choose	ginger
station	chance	
	China	
	rich	
	chin	

6 'h'

Sometimes students tend to put 'h's in where there aren't any. It might be possible to correct this by:

a) finding a similar occurrence in the L1 (e.g. 'heure' in French and 'hour' in English);
b) practising saying the word preceded by, for example, an indefinite article (e.g. an hour, an ear), because, by linking the previous consonant to the vowel (e.g. an (h)our), the 'h' should be omitted.

C ☹

A: Hello, Helen.
B: Hello, Alan. How's Harry?
A: Haven't you heard? He's had an accident in the house.
B: Has he? Is he hurt?
A: Well, he's gone to hospital in an ambulance. Apparently, he's having an operation on his hip.
B: How awful. I hope he's all right.
A: I hope so too.

8 'r' / 'l'

B

1	2	3
red	led	dead
ray	lay	day
row	low	dough
room	loom	doom
reap	leap	deep
rye	lie	die

C ☹

1 Is it right?
2 Look at the grass!
3 What a beautiful lamb!

(a) No, it's wrong.
(a) Yes, I've been gardening.
(b) Ah. It looks very young.

Check your progress 😐

9.15 Mr Arkwright
10.00 Miss Fane
10.30 Mr Booth
11.15 Mrs Witherson
11.45 Miss Ritchley

Dialogue:
A: Can you just run through my appointments for Wednesday?
B: Yes, of course, Mrs Jones. Well, first of all, Mr Arkwright is coming in at 9.15. Then Miss Fane is at 10 o'clock and Mr Booth is after her at 10.30. Then your next appointment is not until 11.15, that's Mrs Witherson, and finally there's Miss Ritchley at 11.45. Is that all right?
A: Yes, that sounds fine, thanks.

Potential problems

1 Difficulties with aspiration of 'p', 't', 'k', e.g. 'bebsi' for 'Pepsi': Arabic, Spanish, Turkish, Chinese, Thai (word final).

2 Difficulties with continuants v. stops, e.g. 'th' / 't'; 'v' / 'b': Arabic, Indonesian, Japanese, Spanish.

3 Difficulties with continuants, e.g. 'th' / 's': French, Spanish, Russian, Arabic, Chinese, Japanese; e.g. 'r' / 'l': Chinese, Japanese, Korean, Thai.

4 Difficulties with affricates, e.g. 'ch' / 'sh', 'j' / 'y': Arabic, Portuguese, Spanish, Thai, French, Scandinavian languages.

24   Sound contrasts – Vowels

This unit aims to help students perceive and, eventually, produce the basic vowel sounds in English.

Again, refer to the 'General guidelines for teaching sound contrasts' in Unit 18 before starting this unit.

Diagnostic test 😀

Use this test as a guide to know which sections of this unit you will need to concentrate on.

1	A	B	C	D
1	live	love	love	love
2	bed	bed	bed	bud
3	ran	ran	run	ran
4	barn	barn	barn	bun
5	hut	hot	hot	hot
6	born	bun	born	born
7	ton	turn	turn	turn
8	room	room	rum	room
9	tale	tale	tale	tell
10	rat	right	right	right
11	join	John	join	join
12	knee	near	near	near
13	very	very	very	vary
14	tow	tow	two	tow
15	hum	home	home	home
16	ground	grand	ground	ground

2 1 Can I have a look at your cut?
    (not 'cat')

 (a) Oh, don't worry, it's nothing
     serious.

   2 Do you need money?
    (not 'many')

 (b) Well ... yes, £10.

   3 Was it caught?
    (not 'cut')

 (a) No, it's still free.

   4 Is it a gull?
    (not 'girl')

 (b) No, it's a pigeon.

5 I need a room.   (a) Certainly, sir, how many nights?
  (not 'rum')

6 He booked me!   (a) Well, there was a no-parking
  (not 'bucked')   sign!

Part 1

A ⌣

This exercise, and the next one, aim at helping students feel the physical difference between vowels, i.e. the articulates of the mouth, tongue and jaw.

The first activity ('tea ... two', etc.) is designed to produce maximum articulation between vowel sounds. If sounds can produce these extremes, they should serve as reference points to find vowel sounds between these points (particularly diphthongs):

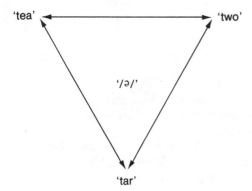

D ⌣

	A	B	C	D
1	feet	feet	<u>fit</u>	feet
2	reach	<u>rich</u>	reach	reach
3	still	<u>steal</u>	still	still
4	<u>teen</u>	tin	tin	tin
5	peach	<u>pitch</u>	peach	peach
6	lick	lick	lick	<u>leak</u>
7	bead	<u>bid</u>	bead	bead

F 😐

1 Where did you slip? (not 'sleep')	(b) On the ice.
2 When did he leave? (not 'live')	(a) At two o'clock.
3 Are you ready, team? (not 'Tim')	(b) Yes, we're all here.

Part 2

Check your progress 😐

1 a
2 i
3 c
4 e
5 d
6 k
7 b

Dialogue:

Tourist officer: Here you are, sir, the bank is in Fane Street.

Tourist: I see. What about the post office, where's that?

Tourist officer: That's in Luck Road ... here.

Tourist: Luck Road. Right. Now, is there a chemist anywhere?

Tourist officer: Yes, I think the biggest one is this one in Tan Lane.

Tourist: Fine. Oh, and is there a public library?

Tourist officer: Yes, of course. It's a very good one. It's in ... Pitt Street, I think ... yes, that's right, Pitt Street.

Tourist: Ah, thank you. And can you tell me where the museum is, I've heard that's very good too.

Tourist officer: Oh, yes, it's definitely worth a visit. It's here, in Royce Lane. Is there anything else you need, sir?

Tourist: I don't think so. Oh, there is one other thing, can you recommend a nice pub for lunch?

Tourist officer: A pub? Let's see. Yes, there's the Red Line in Gray Crescent or there's the Red Lion in St Paul's Square.

Tourist: Marvellous. Well, thank you very much for all your help.

Tourist officer: Not at all, sir. Enjoy your stay.

Tourist: Thank you.

Potential problems

1 Difficulties distinguishing 'Pete' and 'pit': French, Spanish, Japanese, Italian, Turkish.

2 Difficulties distinguishing 'pat' and 'pet': German, Spanish, Arabic, Italian.

3 Difficulties with 'hut': German, French.

4 Difficulties with diphthongs: Italian, French, Greek, Chinese.

5 Difficulties with schwa 'ə': Chinese, Japanese, French, Spanish, Greek.

6 Omission of vowels: Turkish, Arabic.

PART 2: LISTENING
Introduction

This second part of the book concentrates on listening skills, and incorporates a lot of the work done on pronunciation in the first part.

It would be useful to spend some time eliciting some of the points listed under listening 'accurately' and 'efficiently' before moving on to the next section on 'Listening difficulties'.

Listening difficulties

The aim of this section is to focus students' attention on some of the reasons why they have difficulties listening to English, especially natural speech.

It is commonly thought that the main difficulties with listening are caused by lack of vocabulary and speed of speech. While these can obviously cause problems, students need to realise that they are only part of the problem – and often a minor part.

A

This is an introductory exercise for the exercises which follow. You might want to try and elicit possible difficulties from students before looking at this list.

B ⌈··⌉

Students will probably find the second extract, 'Marriage', the easiest to understand.

C ⌈··⌉

Try and elicit from your students why 'Marriage' is probably the easiest before going through the table.

'Marriage' is a dialogue (rather than a group discussion). The subject is probably familiar. Both speakers have fairly standard southern British accents, speak 'clearly', i.e. with frequent pauses, strong stress and focus, clear thought groups, few hesitations and unfinished sentences.

Tapescript

1 'Students in Nice'
   A: The idea is it's supposed to help us a lot with our French. To help us, give us an idea of what it's like to work with the French people and also to help with our management studies.

B: Will any of you come back to France when you've gone back and finished your studies?

C: I want to.

A: Oh yeah. Yes, definitely ...

2 'Marriage'

A: Do you think people go into marriage today thinking they're taking on, though, a very long period of time? I suggest they're perhaps thinking in terms already that there are alternatives even if you do a fairly good stretch like eight years.

B: Well, this has changed of course. I think that what happened is, one of the factors which has contributed to the increasing divorce rate is that as the age of marriage went down and the average age of death went up, it meant that the likely sentence, if I may express it that way, became longer and longer.

3 'Boxing'

A: Cricket it ain't. Tell me about boxing. There's been a lot of criticism recently about people being punch drunk, doing themselves endless injuries, and you're getting a lot of this kind of comment now. What do you say to those people who say that boxing is a dangerous fight, should be taken off, it shouldn't be allowed?

B: I don't really defend it.

Listening test

The Listening test appears at the beginning of this part of the book but can be used, like the Pronunciation test, at different stages, for either diagnostic or progress testing.

It is probably advisable to give the test diagnostically before beginning the Listening units to find out where students have weaknesses, or to skip certain units or sections. Again, the test can be used later on to measure progress.

Each section of the test is designed to test specific listening skills, so, if necessary, go through the terminology and instructions with the students before starting.

This test is recorded on the cassette. If you wish, you may photocopy the pages of the test for students to hand in to you for marking.

Marking: The total score is out of 50.

Tapescript of listening extracts: This can be found on page 82.

Part 1: Listening accuracy

This section is concerned with the ability to recognise individual sounds and words in connected speech, rather than the ability to interpret messages (i.e. comprehension).

A

Marking

There are 7 points for this section, i.e. one each for each correct answer.

Answers

b) a kind of feeling
b) don't you
a) saying
a) wasn't
a) wasn't quite so glamorous
a) that
b) comment

B

Marking

There are 10 points for this section. The points scored should be assessed on the overall percentage of the text which they have written correctly, e.g. 50% = 5 points.

Part 2: Listening comprehension 1

This section tests students' ability to extract key information.

C

Marking

There are 10 points for this section. Check that the student:
– gets the correct information;
– gets the important information (the message is supposed to use the minimum number of words, i.e. the 'content words').

As in Exercise B, the score is based on a percentage.

Answers

To: Eric
From: Joanna
Message: Phone Mr Webster before 5.00 pm re. order sent last Friday.
Tel. no.: 0934 29476

Part 3: Listening comprehension 2

This section tests the students' ability to extract main ideas and follow structure.

D

Marking

There are 6 points for this section, i.e. 2 for each correct answer.

Answers

1 b
2 c
3 b

E

Marking

There are 9 points for this section, i.e. one for each correctly filled gap in the chart.

Answers

Educating foreign children in France

Choice of ....*school*.......... – main factors:

1 *age of child*

2 *parents' perception of two educational traditions*

Recommendations for 'younger child':
French system

because:
easier for child to become bilingual

Recommendations for ....*older*.......... child':
international school system

because:
1 *adjustment to French system is more difficult*

2 *problem of qualifications*

F

Marking

There are 8 points for this section, i.e. 2 for each correct answer.

Answers

'The first is the age of the child and the second is the way the parents perceive what are two very different educational traditions.'

1 The sentence is divided into two parts by a pause between 'child' and 'and'.
2 'Age' is the focus word in the first part.
3 The word 'perceive' is given extra stress to emphasise the importance of the parents' opinion of the two educational traditions.
4 The speaker's voice finished low, because it is the end of an idea.

Tapescript

A

'There must be, for both of you, a kind of feeling, I mean, don't you get a lot of people saying, "Well, boxing and snooker wasn't what it used to be when it wasn't quite so glamorous." Do you get that kind of comment a lot?'

B

'Because both of your sports now are very very, well, I was going to say, snooker perhaps particularly, very dependent on television, or has become er famous because of television. It's important that you get television coverage, is it important what kind of crowd you get there, you know, at the event?'

C

'Oh, hello Eric, it's me, Joanna. Look, I've just had a call from Mr Webster about the order we sent him last Friday. Apparently, it hasn't arrived yet and he's getting a bit upset about it (you know what he's like). It's probably nothing serious but maybe you could check it out and then get in touch with him. I said you'd ring him back this afternoon before five, if that's OK. Oh, by the way, his number is 0934 29476. Cheers! See you tomorrow.'

D

Patrick Middleton, a lecturer in sociology and marketing, is being interviewed about his views on educating foreign children in France.

Alec: ... Patrick, over to you to start with.

Patrick: Well, it seems to me that when parents come down here they've got to make a choice between the French system – state or private – and the international schools, and I think that two factors essentially should weigh in this decision. The first is the age of the child and the second is the way the parents perceive what are two very different educational traditions. Now, as far as the age of the child is concerned, it seems to me that where the younger child is involved, that means up to the age of about eleven, it seems that the balance of advantage is in favour of the French schools. Why? Well, for the younger child it's much easier, I would say, in that context, and there is a fair amount of research which proves this, it's much easier for the child at that age to become bilingual and bicultural, and this is very important. And it's worth stressing that in France that process can start very soon, because France has got the best system of nursery schools in Europe and you can start your child in the nursery school at the age of two and that's a very important experience linguistically and culturally and socially, and especially, I would say, for the foreign child.

Now, once you look at the older child, that's in the sort of pre-teen period and after, the system's rather different, I think, the problem's rather different. First of all, this adjustment to the French system would be much more difficult for the child, linguistically, socially and administratively even. Then, of course, you have the big problem of the child's qualifications for work and for university, perhaps, and it seems to me, at that stage, most parents will in fact opt for the international school.

F

'The first is the age of the child and the second is the way the parents perceive what are two very different educational traditions.'

25 Listening accuracy 1

This unit aims to:

1 Check students' ability to extract the important (i.e. content) words necessary to take a message.
2 Check listening accuracy through dictation.

Both the message-taking activity and the dictation can be done individually, in pairs or as a class activity (writing the message and the dictation on the board).

It is important to alert students to the fact that they may find it difficult to hear words that are reduced.

A ⌐⌐

Suggested notes:

Message from: Jan
Can't meet (lunch) Friday. (Got to go) Manchester. (Possibly) Thursday (instead)? Phone (me) either Tuesday (evening) 6–8 pm – home 981 476 – or Wednesday – work 577 6232.

(The words in brackets could be omitted.)

Tapescript

'Hello. It's me, Jan. / Look, I can't meet you for lunch on Friday. / I've got to go to Manchester for the day. / Could we possibly make it Thursday instead? / If you could phone me / either Tuesday evening / between about six and eight / at my home / the number is nine, eight, one, / four, seven, six. / Or, if not Tuesday evening, / if you could phone me on Wednesday, / at work, / and that number is five, seven, seven, / six, two, / three, two. / Thanks a lot. / Bye.'

26 Listening accuracy 2

This unit aims to help students get key information (particularly numbers) in order to fill in a form.

As the conversation is quite long, it is important for students to concentrate on getting only the information necessary to complete the booking form.

Before listening to the recording, remind students about listening for content and focus words. Also, do some quick oral practice of numbers for revision, if necessary.

C ☺

Holiday reference: S151 02
Departure date: 18th January
No. of nights: 14
Passenger's name: Miss P. Jameson
Address: −
Destination: Barbados
Hotel: Treasure Beach
Accommodation: Twin superior room
Meal plan: Half board
Cost: £1,077 + supplements per person:
     Departure date: £33
     Accommodation: £50
     Meals: £235
     Total price: £2,790 (for two people)

Tapescript

A: Good afternoon, madam. How can I help you?
B: Well, I want to go to Barbados, for two weeks with a girl friend, and I was hoping you could arrange the holiday for me.
A: Yes, certainly. If you just wait a moment I'll get a booking form.
B: Thank you.
A: And we can fill it in. Here we are. Right, now have you seen a brochure?
B: Yes.
A: Do you know the holiday reference number?

B: Yes. Yes, I do. Yes, the number's S151.

A: S151.

B: 02.

A: Fine, and what date would you like to leave on?

B: Oh, hopefully the 18th of January.

A: Right.

B: Yes, it's a Saturday.

A: Ah, right, it'll make a difference. And how long would you like to go for?

B: Fourteen nights.

A: Right. Could I just have your name?

B: Yes, Jameson. J A M E S O N.

A: Jameson. And the initial?

B: P.

A: Is that Mrs or Miss?

B: Miss.

A: And there are two of you?

B: Yes. My friend and I.

A: Right. Fine, and the destination is Barbados.

B: Yes, please.

A: Right. Barbados. Now, would you like to stay in a hotel, an apartment, or a villa?

B: Oh, a hotel.

A: Right. Do you know which hotel?

B: Yes, the Treasure Beach.

A: I've heard that's very nice.

B: Oh, good.

A: Right, now, we have three different classes of room there. There's the 'standard' room, 'superior' room, or what we call a 'deluxe' room.

B: Oh, do you recommend any in particular?

A: Well, deluxe is rather expensive. Actually, I would take a superior, I feel for what, for the money, I think the superior is the best deal.

B: Right. Sort of middle range.

A: Yes.

B: Yes, all right. Thank you.

A: Superior, so superior. Now would that be a double or a twin?

B: A twin.

A: Right, twin superior room. I'm afraid there will be a supplement for that. We'll go through that later on.

B: Right.

A: Now, will you require bed and breakfast, half board or full board?

B: Half board, please.

A: Right. Now I think that's all I need to know. We'll just run through the cost now.

B: Yes.

A: Right.

B: How much is it for each adult?
A: Now, for that hotel at that time of the year, it'll be £1,077 per person. Now there are a few supplements I'm afraid.
B: Yes.
A: The date you want to leave is a Saturday and there'll be a £33 per person supplement for that.
B: Right, can I just write that down?
A: Yes, that's £33 for the Saturday departure.
B: Yes. That's per person?
A: Per person, yes. For the superior twin there is a £50 per person supplement.
B: Yes. Right.
A: And then for the half board it's another £235 per person. The cost is just for the room, that's stated in the brochure.
B: I see, yes, 235.
A: 235, yes.
B: Is that each?
A: That's each, yes.
B: Right.
A: So if we add all that up it comes to ... let's see ... 2,790. That's the total price.
B: OK.
A: And we can guarantee it won't be any more than that.
B: I hope not!

D

27 Getting key information 1

This unit aims to help students select and note key information.

There are three announcements: the first is at an airport, the second at a railway station and the third on a train. Make sure the students look through the charts and are familiar with the vocabulary before listening to the recordings. Try and get the students to fill in the charts after listening only once to the complete announcement, to encourage them to listen only for key information.

A ☐

BRITISH AIRWAYS: Departures
Flight no.: BA607
Destination: Oslo
Departure time: 15.45
Delay: Due to weather conditions

Passenger instructions:
1 Wait in International Departure Lounge.
2 Contact Information Desk for onward connections.

Tapescript

'British Airways regret to announce the delay of flight BA607 to Oslo, due to adverse weather conditions. The estimated departure time is now 15.45. Passengers are requested to wait in the International Departure Lounge until the flight is called. Any passengers with onward connections should contact the Information Desk in the Departure Lounge. We regret any inconvenience caused to passengers.'

B ☐

ARRIVALS   DEPARTURES
Time: 11.16   Time: 17.55
To: London   To: Edinburgh
Platform: 14   Platform: 7

Tapescript

'The train now approaching platform 14 is the 11.16 to London, Euston.
    Your attention, please. This is a platform alteration. The 17.55 train to Edinburgh, due to depart from platform 10, will now leave from platform 7. This train will stop at Darlington, Durham and Newcastle.'

C ⊡

1 True
2 False
3 True
4 False

Tapescript

'Ladies and gentlemen. This is the Chief Steward speaking. There is a buffet service on this train. The buffet car is situated at the rear of first class and at the front of second class and is now open for the sale of hot and cold snacks, licensed and soft drinks. Passengers are advised that the buffet will be closing in 20 minutes' time. Thank you.'

28 Getting key information 2

This unit aims to help students select key information from extracts of natural speech. The recorded material is 'live' interviews with British Rail staff at York Railway Station.

A

This is a good opportunity for students to practise using their dictionaries to find new words. Make sure they check the pronunciation of new vocabulary before listening to the recording. The activity of listening for particular words in a recording is especially useful for students with weak comprehension skills, and it can help increase confidence and motivation.

B

Before listening to the recording elicit from students what sort of difficulties they would have when trying to understand English in a situation like a busy railway station. (Refer back to some of the points on 'Listening difficulties' on page 107 in the Student's Book if necessary.)

1 e
2 b
3 c
4 h

C ⌣

1 'Excuse me. Could you tell me …?'
2 'Excuse me. Is there …?'

D ⊡

1 Yes, as you're facing the station, it's on the left-hand side.
2 Yes, certainly. If you go out of the station, turn to your left. Follow the road down to the traffic lights. You'll see it on the right-hand side.

Tapescript

(I = Interviewer)

I: Excuse me. Could you tell me if there's a ladies' toilet in the station?
— Yes, there is a ladies' toilet, just go out through the door where it says trains and turn to the right and it's just directly in front of you.
I: Thanks very much.
— OK.

I: Excuse me. Is there a left luggage office in the station?
— Yes, if you go through the barrier, turn left, it's on platform 2.
I: Platform 2. Thank you.

I: Excuse me. Is there a car park near the station?
— Yes, as you're facing the station, it's on the left-hand side.
I: Is it very far?
— No, just next door.
I: Thank you.

I: Excuse me. Could you tell me where the bus station is?
— Yes, certainly. If you go out of the station, turn to your left. Follow the road down to the traffic lights. You'll see it on the right-hand side.
I: Thanks. Is it very far?
— No. It'll take you about three minutes to walk, that's all.
I: Right. Thank you.
— OK. Thank you. Bye-bye.

29 Review

This unit aims to review the main points in the four previous units:
1 Listening accurately;
2 Getting key information.

The recorded material consists of individual interviews with the three people about their jobs.

A

As in the previous unit, use this exercise for dictionary and pronunciation accuracy practice.

B

Ann-Marie's present job: print maker and painter (photos 2 and 6)
John's present job: actor (photo 4)
Dave's present job: recording engineer (photo 1)

C ⌐⊡¬

1 She works in a studio in the university.
  She has done this job in York for twelve years.
  She was an English teacher in Sweden for a year.
2 'I taught English / in Sweden / for a year.'

D ⌐⊡¬

1 John said: 'I work on a freelance basis.'
  i.e. he is self-employed. (c)
2 He acts mostly on the stage. (a)
3 He prefers acting on the stage because he gets feedback from the audience.

E [cassette icon]

1 He has been in his present job for two years.
Before that he was a musician, and played the guitar and bass guitar.
He has made a few records and been on television a lot.
2 a) The first stressed word is 'recording'.
  b) 'I'm a reCORding engiNEER.'
3 'You're interested in the technical side of it?'
  'Yes, as well as the musical side.'

Tapescript

(I = Interviewer; AM = Ann-Marie)

I: Ann-Marie, what exactly do you do?
AM: I'm a print maker and a painter.
I: Uh uh. And do you do that professionally then?
AM: Yes, I do it professionally.
I: Where do you work?
AM: Um, I've got a studio, in the university.
I: So you live in the university, do you?
AM: Yes.
I: And how long have been doing this sort of work?
AM: Well, I've been in York about twelve years (uh uh) and I've been, I
    was a post-graduate student before that. So, I suppose, about sixteen
    years.
I: And what did you do before that?
AM: Um, I taught English, in Sweden.
I: Really?
AM: For a year. Yes.
I: Did you learn any Swedish?
AM: A bit, yes.
I: Ah, good. OK.

(J = John)
I: John, what exactly do you do?
J: Er, well, I'm an actor.
I: Uh uh.
J: And I work with, on a freelance basis, so I'm working with different
   companies, when the opportunity arises, basically.
I: What sort of acting. On the stage?
J: Er, yeah.
I: Have you lived in York very long?
J: Um, I came up to study drama at a college in York, in 1977, so I've
   been here ever since then.
I: Er, have you ever worked in, in film?

J: Um, I did a, I've done a bit of TV, er on a soap opera, which was, er, quite interesting but it actually gets very boring 'cos you're hanging (does it?) around for a long time waiting.

I: Is it a different technique for television, acting?

J: Er.

I: Which do you think you prefer?

J: Oh, I am, I prefer the live performance (yes, yes), um, because it changes all the time as to what type of audience you've got.

I: Mm, it's more exciting probably.

J: Er, and you get the feedback from the audience.

I: Yes, yeah. Fine. Thank you, John.

(D = Dave)

I: Dave, what exactly do you do?

D: I'm a recording engineer.

I: Yes.

D: Yes.

I: What sort of work do you get involved in?

D: Um, mainly bands, recording erm groups, er voices, sound effects, er but most, most of the work is in recording groups.

I: And do you end up with the finished product?

D: Yes.

I: Yeah, so you take the work from the beginning to the end?

D: Yes.

I: Yeah? How long have you been doing this sort of work?

D: Er, two years now.

I: Two years. And what did you do before that?

D: Before that, I was a musician.

I: Really! What, what instrument do you play?

D: Guitar and bass guitar.

I: Ah. Is that how you became interested in recording?

D: Yes. I, I also worked in electronics, and, er, I worked on the audio side, and, um, I basically wanted to get into recording.

I: You're interested in the technical side of it?

D: Yes, as well, as well as the musical side.

I: Yeah. Do you still play your guitar?

D: Yes.

I: Professionally?

D: Yes.

I: Ah. Have you made any recordings of yourself?

D: Er, I've been on a few records. I've been on television a lot.

I: Great.

30 Taking notes 1

This unit aims to guide students towards structuring notes clearly and concisely using specific listening skills (i.e. selecting main ideas and following the structure of talk).

Distinguishing between main points and supporting ideas is extremely difficult for some students. This may be because the structure of talk can be subject to cultural differences. Some societies place a very high value on analytical, sequential presentations of ideas. Other societies place more value on formulaic speech, using fixed expressions that are combined to emphasise shared feeling. This can produce a very different sense of what is important in narrative (Tannen, 1981).

Before listening to the talk you may want to guide the students by eliciting answers to these questions:

1 Why is skill at note taking important? (for studying, recording meetings, etc.)
2 Why should you not try to write every word? (not enough time, will miss bits of talk, etc.)
3 What words are most important? (new information, focus words)
4 How can you recognise these words? (intonation, focus, pauses)

A

Three reasons.
Three skills.

B

Reason for taking notes: To remember the structure and content of something you hear, e.g. a meeting or lecture

Difficulties in taking notes:
1 Understanding individual words and sounds
2 Different structure of talk in different languages
3 Difficult to write and listen at same time

Important skills to help take better notes:
1 Listen for and note content words, i.e. important/new information

2 Listen for structure signals (e.g. 'finally', 'however') and pronunciation signals (e.g. pitch, pause)
3 Invent a notation system (e.g. numbering, different print)

C ⊡

When you have gone over Exercise B, pick out part of the talk to do as a short dictation and to analyse elements such as content and focus words and pitch change. For example:

There are ↑ THREE imPORtant skills you can deVElop to HELP you TAKE BETTER NOTES IN ENGLISH ↓

Tapescript

'Sometimes it is necessary to take notes about the structure and content of what you hear, to remind yourself, or someone else, afterwards; for example, after a meeting or a lecture. However, it is not easy to take good notes in a foreign language, partly because you may have difficulties understanding individual words or sounds and partly because the structure of the talk may be different in your own language. Moreover, it is difficult to write and listen at the same time – if you try to write every word you will probably end up either with confusing notes or missing what is being said.

There are three important skills you can develop to help you take better notes in English. First of all, listen for the most important words. Significant words are usually the ones that give new information and are often the 'focus' of a phrase or sentence. They are usually emphasised by a pitch movement and this signals their importance. Content words, like nouns and verbs, are often the focus of infor-mation, therefore notes should be almost entirely made up of content words – not whole sentences. So remember, you need information, not sentences.

Secondly, try and follow the structure of the talk by listening for specific phrases which signal the sequence of ideas, for example, 'first of all', 'and now I'd like to move on to ...', and 'finally ...' and which signal the connection between ideas, for example, 'however ...' 'on the other hand ...', 'in addition ...'. Listen also for specific pronunciation elements, such as pauses and pitch change which tell you when a speaker has finished talking about one topic, by using low pitch and a pause, and is about to start a new one, using high pitch to signal important information.

Thirdly, try and invent your own system of notation, such as using numbers or different sorts of print to highlight different points, to organise your notes clearly so that you can read them easily later. So if you use these three signals – picking out important words, following the structure of the talk and using a system of notation, you should be able to make concise, useful notes.'

31 Taking notes 2

This unit aims to:
1 Practise selecting important ideas as a guide to taking notes.
2 Practise using phonological clues such as pitch change, pauses, focus, etc. to hear the structure of a talk.

A

Before listening to the talk, focus the students' attention by eliciting some possible reasons for the variation in pronunciation achievement.

B ▦

1 c
2 a
3 c

C ▦

Before starting this, remind students of the techniques for taking notes outlined in Unit 30.

Notes can either be taken individually or in pairs or groups. Here are some suggestions:
— Students start to take notes individually. Halfway through the talk, ask the class to dictate the main points for you, or another student, to write on the board. Check that they have a clear idea of the subject, i.e. the main idea and supporting ideas. Continue in sections, deciding on a notation system and a conclusion.
— 'Reverse-construction' This is a technique which helps sharpen note-taking skills. Ask students to compare their notes with partners, as a preparation for reconstructing the lecture. If students can recreate their own version of the lecture using their own notes it shows that they have recorded the main points clearly. One team should be responsible for the first part of the talk, another for the next part and so on.

Students will develop their own method of note taking and their own judgement of what material must be recorded, so the class discussions about notes should not have a correct/incorrect emphasis. The purpose is to stimulate individual analytical thinking and active choice.

Tapescript

'Today's short lecture then is on the subject of Pronunciation Achievement Factors.

Perhaps as an introduction we should ask ourselves three questions. Why should it be difficult for adults to learn accurate pronunciation in a foreign language? Secondly, why should some people achieve better results than others? And thirdly, what factors predict who will achieve good pronunciation?

There have been research studies identifying several factors which might affect performance. Suter, the American language researcher, found four significant factors. Firstly, and perhaps the most significant, was the mother tongue. The closer the student's own language was to English to start with, the greater the chance of high achievement. Secondly, he discovered the attitude to pronunciation. It makes a difference if the student believes in the importance of pronunciation. Thirdly, conversation with natives – the amount of time spent talking to native English speakers. Fourth, and possibly the least important, was the student's own natural or innate ability. The ability to imitate helps, but not nearly as much as people think. It's far less significant than the other three factors. Two others were tested but found to be of little overall value. Firstly, the sex of the student and secondly, the personality – whether he was introverted or extroverted, outgoing or shy.

So to draw a conclusion. Well, we can't change the first factor, the mother tongue, but we can control the second and third. Therefore, we have a considerable choice in improving the student's own pronunciation learning.'

32 Following structure

This unit aims to help students consider the structure of oral presentations and the importance of phonological items such as thought groups, focus and pitch change for clear structure.

There are two versions of a presentation about Clifton Language Training, a private language training company. It is important that students focus as much as possible on the structure of the presentations rather than the content.

B

This could be a brainstorming session, listing on the board as many criteria as possible for making a good oral presentation. The aim, at this stage, is merely to list points rather than evaluate them in depth. The points can be reconsidered after listening to the presentations.

C

These are general comprehension questions. It is important that students feel they have 'understood' the content before looking at the structure of the talks.

1 An English language training consultancy
2 In the north of England
3 Five
4 English for Specific Purposes
5 a) courses in Clifton (one-to-one, two-to-one and small groups)
  b) courses abroad (mainly groups)
6 Write materials
7 a) needs analysis
  b) design course
  c) run course
  d) suggest follow-up
  e) evaluation

D 😐

The questions in the checklist are to guide students' attention to:
a) the structure of the presentation;
b) the speech.

The first question is important to get an overall impression of the clarity of the presentation, especially in terms of structure and speech.

Question two refers to both the length of the talk and the density of information.

Question three refers to the clarity of the structure of the talk:
a) the global structure;
b) the use of signals, e.g. 'firstly', 'next', 'finally', to mark the sequence.

Question four looks at the actual speech:
a) the phonological items such as focus, stress, pauses and pitch;
b) use of hesitations and fillers;
c) volume and speed (was it too loud or quiet, or too fast or slow?).

Listener's checklist

	Yes	*OK*	*No*
1 Did the speaker make it easy for the listener to understand?	2		1
2 Was the amount of information correct?		1 / 2	
3 *Structure* a) Was there an 'introduction', 'middle' and 'conclusion'? b) Was there a clear sequence to help predict what would come next?	2 2		1 1

4 *Speech*
a) Were there clear:
  – focus words / stress?
  – thought groups / pauses?
  – pitch changes?
b) Were there many hesitations and 'fillers'?
c) Was there correct:
  – volume?
  – speed?
	
	2
	2
	2
	1
	
		1
		
		1
		
		1 / 2
		1 / 2
			
			1
			
			2

E 🔛

This exercise concentrates on the second set of criteria in the checklist, i.e. speech. It illustrates the use of pauses and stress. Both extracts are repeated on the cassette after the presentations.

'so FIRstly / WHAT is CLIFton LANguage TRAINing / well / it's an ENGlish LANguage TRAINing consULtancy BAsed in CLIFton / in the NORTH of ENgland / it was esTABlished in 1980 with the obJEctive of SPEcialising in INDustry-speCIfic LANguage TRAINing / there are PRINcipally TWO MAIN acTIVities'

Tapescript

Presentation 1
'I'd like to talk to you about Clifton Language Training. I don't know if any of you have heard of it, but what we're into is ESP, that's English for Specific Purposes.

There are five partners in it, er, that is four teaching partners and one administrative partner, and we started in about 1980 with the idea of specialising in industry-specific language training. What do we mean by industry-specific language training? Well, we try to do an analysis of needs of the company or of the student and, on this basis, go on to design a course. We have essentially two main activities, um, we run courses in Clifton, either individual courses or group courses. An individual course would be on the basis of one teacher to one student and, er, a group course might be one teacher to four or five students, and we also do courses abroad.

Um, to get back to what I was saying, we, we do an analysis of the needs of the students and then go on to design the course, and of course then teach the course, and in teaching the course, it's very important to develop good materials, based on the students' needs and using the resources that we have available in print, audio and video.

Er, while I'm talking about materials, you might also be interested to know that we develop materials for publishers and we also develop materials specially commissioned by companies.

So, um that's something about what we do: the two main activities … Well, I can't think of anything else to say. I think that's just about it, really. Are there any questions?'

Presentation 2
'Good morning, ladies and gentlemen. I'd like to talk to you, very briefly, about Clifton Language Training. And what I'll try to cover is: what is Clifton Language Training, who is in it, and how we work.

So, firstly, what is Clifton Language Training? Well, it's an English language training consultancy, based in Clifton, in the north of England. It was established in 1980, with the objective of specialising in industry-specific language training.

There are principally two main activities. Firstly, in Clifton, we run individual courses of two types, either what we call a 'one-to-one', that is one teacher for one student, or a 'two-to-one', two teachers for one student. And we also run small group courses in Clifton. The other main activity, our overseas services, where we send a trainer abroad to work on-site, usually with a group, in a company.

In addition to these two main activities, we also write a lot of materials, both for publishers and also specially commissioned by companies.

So, let's move on now, to who is in it. There are five partners, four teaching partners and one administrative partner and, in addition, there are several, experienced freelance teachers.

And, finally, we come on to how do we work. And here I'd like to stress that, as a partnership, we are not only a partnership amongst ourselves, but we also are partners for our clients, and the basis for all the work we do is a very thorough needs analysis, that is an analysis of the job-related communication needs of the students. On the basis of this analysis, we go on to design a course and then to actually run the course. Now, obviously, an integral part of the course itself are the materials and for the development of these materials we call on our extensive resources of print, audio and video material.

And, finally, at the end of the course, there will be suggestions for follow-up and a thorough evaluation in terms of the objectives set during the needs analysis.

So, very briefly, that hopefully answers three questions: what is Clifton Language Training, who is in it, and, thirdly, how do we work.

Are there any questions you'd like to ask?'

33   Keeping track

This unit aims to help students to 'keep track', i.e. follow the ideas and structure of a discussion, by:
1 Selecting key information from a group of people talking naturally (with distractions such as speaking at the same time, unfinished remarks, etc.).
2 Using strategies such as concentrating on interviewer's questions to predict key information.

The recording is part of a radio interview with a group of British and American students studying at the University of Nice, in France. They are giving their opinions about living and studying in France.

B

Again, this could be a brainstorming activity, listing all possible advantages, and disadvantages on the board. The aim is to direct the students' listening.

C

1 Yes
2 Yes
3 No

D

Possible sentence endings:

1 'Compared to the length of time we studied in England and how much we improved there, it's amazing how much we've learnt here.'
2 'It's the only way to do it really, to become really fluent in a language you have to live in the country.'
3 'Do you think France is an easier place to live than Britain (I'll ask the Brits first and then the Americans) at the moment? I mean, do you think it's easier to do certain things here?'

E 🔲

1 'Will any of you come back to France when you've gone back and finished your studies?' (*getting information*)
2 'Would you like to come and work here on a permanent basis?' (*getting information*)
3 'How about the language? Are your, has your French come on a lot since you've been here?' (*getting information*)
4 'You're all pretty fluent now, are you?' (*checking information*)
5 'Do you think France is an easier place to live than Britain (I'll ask the Brits first and then the Americans) at the moment?' (*getting information*)

Refer students back to Unit 16 if necessary.

Tapescript

(I = Interviewer)

I: Will any of you come back to France when you've gone back and finished your studies?
– I want to.
– Oh yeah. Yes, definitely ...
I: Would you like to come and work here on a permanent basis?
– ... the climate mainly ...
I: How about the language? Are your, has your French come on a lot since you've been here?
– Yes. Definitely. Yeah.
I: You're all pretty fluent now, are you?
– Compared to the length of time we studied in England and how much we improved there, it's amazing ...
– It's the only way to do it really, to become really fluent in a language ...
– You're taught out of a book, grammar book, up until the age of about eighteen and then when you're sent abroad that's the actual practice you get, and that's what actually makes you progress.
– I think we've spoken more French in the two months that we've been here than we did in the six years prior, studying from a book in a classroom.
I: Do you think France is an easier place to live than Britain (I'll ask the Brits first and then the Americans) at the moment? I mean, do you think it's ...?
– I think it's more difficult. Just, just the organisation of everything is more difficult.
– Yeah, it's more difficult. You have to organise yourself a lot more ...
– Yeah.
– ... in order to get to places, in order to sort things out, in order to get things done. Because things take time. Yeah.

34 Review

This unit reviews some of the main elements of the Listening units:
1 Listening accurately
2 Getting key information
3 Following structure ⎫ taking notes
4 Keeping track ⎭

The recording is part of a radio interview with Patrick Middleton, a lecturer in sociology. He is giving his views about marriage.

C 😐

The main point is (b). The other points exemplify this fact.

D 😐

Main idea:	Marriage is changing, especially in terms of length
Supporting ideas:	e.g. 100 years ago marriage lasted about 25 years because
	a) people married later
	b) people died earlier
	Marriage was different,
	i.e. shorter with more children,
	therefore, too busy to recognise problems

Main idea:	Factors contributing to increasing divorce rate:
	age of marriage went down
	age of death went up
	therefore longer marriage
Supporting ideas:	e.g. today:
	average age at marriage – 22–23
	average age at death – close to 80
	average length of marriage – 50–60 years

E ⌣

The thought groups are short.
The pauses are frequent and often long.
The focus words are emphasised strongly.
His voice falls at the end of ideas.

The extract is repeated on the cassette at the end of the interview.

'I think the <u>first</u> mistake that people make is to <u>imagine</u> that the word "<u>marriage</u>" ↓ / represents a constant <u>reality</u> ↑ / er that hasn't <u>changed</u> ↓ / and of course it <u>has</u> changed ↑ / and I think the most <u>important</u> way it's changed ↑ / is in terms of its <u>length</u> ↓ '

Tapescript

Patrick: I think the first mistake that people make is to imagine that the word 'marriage' represents a constant reality, er that hasn't changed. And of course it has changed and I think the most important way it's changed is in terms of its length. Let's imagine that you married exactly a hundred years ago. Well, at that time, you had in front of you, if you had the average marriage, you had about twenty-five years. Of course, sometimes more but sometimes less. This was because people married later. It's worth mentioning, I think, that one thing people often don't know is that until the early part of this century, I'd say round about 1920, most people got married later than twenty-five, after twenty-five rather than before. Then of course, they died earlier, so this meant that the section of life available for marriage was much shorter. Now, this meant, of course, that when you married, you were faced with a very different prospect from today. It was a shorter period with far more children. Again, exactly a hundred years ago the average completed family was six children and that meant they were too busy to have the sort of problems which sometimes create divorce.

Interviewer: Do you think people go into marriage today thinking they're taking on, though, a very long period of time? I suggest they're perhaps thinking in terms already that there are alternatives even if you do a fairly good stretch like eight years.

Patrick: Well, this has changed, of course. I think that what happened is, one of the factors which has contributed to the increasing divorce rate is that as the age of marriage went down and the average age of death went up, it meant that the likely sentence, if I may express it that way, became longer and longer. For example, if you marry today, at the age, let's say of twenty-two, twenty-three, the age is rising at the moment actually slightly, but this is more or less the average, and you live for the normal life span, which means you're likely to come close up to eighty in many cases, you face a sentence of what, fifty, fifty-five even sixty years. This is a very unattractive prospect.

35 Student's dictation

The last two units in the book are production-oriented activities where the student is free to choose his or her own input.

The activities are designed to consolidate work done in the Pronunciation and Listening units of the book.

The aim here is to analyse 'communication breakdown' in terms of:
a) speaker's errors;
b) listener's errors.
Explain to the students that the dictation is not just a listening test, but should help everyone identify weaknesses in speaking as well as listening.

Note:
1 This exercise is more likely to be successful with a multi-lingual class. If the class is mono-lingual they usually understand each other's English because they make the same mistakes.
2 Students sometimes express doubts about the value of taking dictation from a non-native speaker. Point out that it is just as important to understand and be understood by non-native speakers as by native speakers.

Procedure

If possible, get students to record the dictation rather than read it aloud. The advantage is that the recording is consistent, especially in terms of phonological features such as pitch change, pause and stress.

Take down the dictation yourself while the students are writing. Note all the errors you can. In particular, errors in stress and thought groups may not be noticed by the class, so you will need to record them.

Analysis

Content words: If a content word is faulty or missing the confusion may extend for several words following, while the listener is trying to identify the missing word. Also, the error may cause a mistaken idea later as the listener tries to make sense of the sentence (e.g. if the noun is thought to be a verb, or vice versa).

Syllables: Syllables are frequently dropped, either in unstressed prefixes or (more commonly) in final syllables. Final 's' is the most common error.

Sounds: Individual sound errors often fall into categories of the stop/ continuant contrast or the voiced/unvoiced contrast.

It is not always easy to tell if an error was a speaking mistake or a listening mistake, but some patterns are easily recognisable. For instance, if a speaker pronounced 'of' as 'off' it is likely that the student will write it that way. This is a speaker error, not a listener error. On the other hand, if you know that the speaker said 'present' and several students wrote 'pleasant', you can point it out as a listener error.

Unfamiliar words: If there was an unfamiliar idiom or word, it may have caused confusion or been missed. Point out the importance of pronouncing such words very clearly, possibly with a short pause before and afterwards.

If you are a native speaker of English and an experienced teacher of the language, your ear will have a tendency to filter out and correct errors automatically; in this case, the non-native speaker may have an advantage, in being more critical.

Analysis of these dictations can provide a practical summary of everything you have taught the students in this course. After the analysis, and some class practice of the sentences, the students can record the dictation again, for comparison with the original version.

36   Student's oral presentation

The aim is to develop self-assessment of oral communication from:
a) the speaker's point of view;
b) the listener's point of view.

As with Unit 35, explain that this activity is not just a speaking test but should focus attention on listening as well as speaking weaknesses and strengths.

Procedure

1 Be strict about the time allowance. It promotes more careful planning if the speaker knows the time is limited.
2 Make sure students only prepare notes, not a complete script (refer them back to Units 30 and 31 if necessary).
3 Encourage students to choose 'interesting' subjects in respect of their audience. Presentations are generally much more effective if the audience feel they are learning something new.
4 Make sure that both speaker and listeners are aware of their respective responsibility, i.e. to be understood and to understand.
   One way to do this is to ask everyone to refer to the 'Listener's checklist' (Unit 32) before they start. As well as asking listeners to complete the 'Listener's checklist' or to take notes during the talk, another way to encourage the audience to listen critically is to get one or two students during each presentation to:
a) prepare three questions about the talk;
b) write a summary of the main points.

The purpose of all these activities is to focus attention on the effectiveness of the presentation.

Further-study guide

As with any sort of language course, it is important for students to continue studying on their own afterwards.

There are suggestions in the Student's Book to help guide students who want to continue working on their own pronunciation (both for speech, i.e. 'Production', and listening, i.e. 'Recognition').

Reference can also be made to some of the suggestions in the section on 'Integrating pronunciation teaching' on page ix of this book.

Bibliography

Adams, Corinne, *English Speech Rhythm and the Foreign Learner*, Mouton, 1979.

Baker, Ann, *Ship or Sheep*, Cambridge University Press, 1981.

Baker, Ann, *Tree or Three*, Cambridge University Press, 1982.

Bolinger, Dwight L., *Forms of English*, Harvard University Press, 1961.

Brazil, David, Coulthard, Malcolm, and Johns, Catherine, *Discourse Intonation and Language Teaching*, Longman, 1980.

Brown, Gillian, *Listening to Spoken English*, Longman, 1977.

Brown, Gillian, and Currie, Karen L., *Questions of Intonation*, Croom Helm, 1980.

Brown, Gillian, and Yule, George, *Teaching the Spoken Language*, Cambridge University Press, 1983.

Cruttenden, Alan, *Intonation*, Cambridge University Press, 1986.

Crystal, David, *Prosodic Systems and Intonation in English*, Cambridge University Press, 1969.

Crystal, David, *The English Tone of Voice*, Edward Arnold, 1975.

Gilbert, Judy B., 'Pronunciation, an aid to listening comprehension', *CATESOL Occasional Papers*, 8: 62–71, 1982.

Gimson, A. C., *An Introduction to the Pronunciation of English*, Edward Arnold, 1980.

Graham, Carolyn, *Jazz Chants*, Oxford University Press, 1978.

Gumperz, John, and Kaltman, Hannah, 'Prosody, linguistic diffusion and conversational inference', *Berkeley Linguistic Society*, 6: 44–65, 1980.

Hubicka, O., 'Why bother about phonology?', *Practical English Teaching*, I/1, 1980.

Huggins, A. W. F., 'Some effects on intelligibility of inappropriate temporal relations within speech units', *Proceedings of the Ninth International Congress of Phonetic Sciences*, Vol. 12, University of Copenhagen, Institute of Phonetics, 1979.

Kenworthy, Joanne, *Teaching English Pronunciation*, Longman, 1987.

Leahy, R., 'A practical approach for teaching ESL pronunciation based on distinctive feature analysis', *TESOL Quarterly*, 14: 209–306, 1980.

MacCarthy, Peter, *The Teaching of Pronunciation*, Cambridge University Press, 1978.

Mortimer, Colin, *Elements of Pronunciation*, Cambridge University Press, 1985.

O'Connor, J. D., *Better English Pronunciation*, Cambridge University Press, 1980.

Roach, Peter, *English Phonetics and Phonology*, Cambridge University Press, 1983.

Sacks, H., Schegloff, E. and Jefferson, G., 'A simplest systematics for the organisation of turn-taking in conversations', *Language*, 50, 1974.

Swan, Michael, and Smith, Bernard (eds), *Learner English*, Cambridge University Press, 1987.

Tannen, Deborah, 'Implications of the oral/literate continuum for cross-cultural communication', *Georgetown University Round Table on Languages and*

Linguistics 1080: Current Issues in Bilingualism, J. Alatis (ed.), Georgetown University Press, 1981.

Thompson, Ian, *Intonation Practice*, Oxford University Press, 1982.

Tomatis, L. A., *L'integration des langues vivantes*, Société Soditap, Paris, 1966.